GENESIS FOR TEENS

Andrew Gad

SAINT **SHENOUDA** PRESS

GENESIS FOR TEENS

by

Andrew Gad

ST SHENOUDA'S PRESS
SYDNEY, AUSTRALIA
2020

GENESIS FOR TEENS

ST SHENOUDA PRESS
8419 Putty Rd,
Putty, NSW, 2330

www.stshenoudapress.com

ISBN 13: 978-0-6488658-7-2

About the Author:

Dr Andrew Gad is a Sunday School servant at St Mary and St Mina's Coptic Orthodox Church, Sydney, NSW. He works as a doctor and he enjoys reading commentaries of the fathers and teaching young teens in Sunday School.

Cover Design:
Mariana Hanna
In and Out Creation Pty Ltd
inandoutcreations.com.au

Text Layout:
Hani Ghaly,
Begoury Graphics
begourygraphics@gmail.com

CONTENTS

WHY STUDY GENESIS?

The word "genesis" comes from the Hebrew word meaning origin or beginning. So the book of Genesis is a book of beginnings. It is the first book in the Bible, recounting the creation of the world, the fall of Adam and Eve, God's covenant to mankind and the origin of the house of Israel.

The book of Genesis is filled with many themes relevant to society today, love, hatred, greed, jealousy, violence and sexual sins. In this book, we learn about a range of different people who wrestled with God to find success, love and happiness in a world gone wrong. They suffer and then succeed. They do right, and then do wrong. With God's help, sometimes they fight their way to a happy ending. And God uses their struggles, their suffering and their choices (both bad and good) to allow them to return and come back to Him.

In this book, we will go through Genesis character by character and story by story. We'll meet people who are just like us; some who are close to God and would to anything to please Him, and others who feel disappointed, betrayed and helpless, with no real relationship with God. There is a lesson to be learnt in every single chapter and from every single character!

INTRODUCTION

WHO WROTE GENESIS?

Moses is the author of Genesis. He was a prophet, called by God to lead the children of Israel from their captivity in Egypt all the way to the promised land of Canaan (See the book of Exodus). Because Moses was not around during the events of Genesis, he did not learn about them firsthand. Rather, he was inspired by the Holy Spirit and also the several historical sources which were available to him.

It's important to realise that Moses himself was not perfect. For starters, he had a stutter (Exod 4:10) and did not consider himself fit to lead the people of Israel. At one stage he even argued and pleaded with God for someone else to take the responsibility (Exod 4:13). Even during his ministry, Moses doubted and disobeyed God on several occasions, even committing murder when attempting to resolve a conflict (Exod 2:11-12). So God does not expect us to be perfect, but accepts our short-comings and just wants us to repent and turn back to Him.

WHEN AND WHERE WAS GENESIS WRITTEN?

There are varying opinions on when Genesis and the other books of Moses were written, but most scholars agree that it was written between the 15th and 13th centuries BC. Unfortunately, we don't know exactly where Moses was at the time of writing.

WHAT'S UNIQUE ABOUT GENESIS?

Genesis serves as an introduction to the other books of Moses (Exodus, Leviticus, Numbers and Deuteronomy), as well as the entire Old Testament. It provides the Old Testament's only record of many important events, such as the Creation, Fall of Adam and Eve, The Flood and The establishment of the Abrahamic Covenant. However, only 11 chapters of Genesis are dedicated to the time from the creation of Earth to Abraham, with the remaining 39 chapters dedicated to the life of Abraham, Isaac, Jacob and Jacob's sons. This suggests that Moses desired to teach the children of Israel about the covenants the Lord made with their forefathers, to demonstrate to them how blessed they were in the eyes of God.

A QUICK OUTLINE

Genesis 1-4: Moses describes the creation of the Earth and all living things upon it. Meanwhile, Adam and Eve eat of the forbidden tree and are cast out of the Garden of Eden. They give birth to children (Cain, Abel and many others), and Cain kills Abel.

Genesis 5-11: Because of the wickedness of mankind, God promises to flood the earth. Noah follows God's commandments to build an ark, and his family as well as the whole animal population is saved. After mankind tries to build the Tower of Babel (in order to reach God), God confuses the people by making them speak in different languages.

Genesis 12-23: God promises Abram that he will become great nation and have descendants like the sand of the sea. God changes Abram's name to Abraham after making a covenant with him. The land of Sodom and Gomorrah is destroyed, and only Abraham's nephew Lot is saved. Abraham has a child Isaac, who he is willing to sacrifice in accordance with God's instruction.

Genesis 24-36: Isaac marries Rebekah, and they have two children- Esau and Jacob. Esau sells his birthright to Jacob, causing Esau to hate Jacob and plan on killing him. God protects Jacob and gives him the same promise he gave his father Abraham. Jacob and Esau reconcile, and Jacob has twelve sons.

Genesis 37-50: Joseph is favoured by his father Jacob. Because of this, Joseph's brothers hate him and sell him as a slave into Egypt. After being thrown into prison and facing many hardships, Joseph works his way to becoming second in charge of Egypt. Eventually, Joseph and his brothers reconcile.

CHAPTER 1

IN THE BEGINNING

Events

CHAPTER 1

Moses chooses to start off the book of Genesis exactly the same way St. John the evangelist began his gospel many thousands of years later. While John starts off his recap of the New Testament with 'In the beginning was the Word and the Word was with God and the Word was God' (John 1:1), Moses uses the first sentence of the entire Bible to exclaim 'In the beginning God created the heavens and the earth' (Genesis 1:1).

From the beginning of the creation, the presence of the Holy Trinity is obvious. In verse 1, the Hebrew translation for God is 'Elohim', plural for 'Elih' which means God. This is to confirm and establish that the Trinity existed from the beginning of time, and not just God the Father.

But why does Moses keep repeating: "then God said" time and time again throughout the chapter? This is not a physical voice or word of mouth, since God the Father did not speak these words out loud. Rather, this refers to the Jesus Christ the Son (the Logos, also known as the Word of God) through which all creation took place. In verse 2, "the spirit of God was hovering over the waters", indicating the presence of the Holy Spirit as well. The unity of the Holy Trinity is summed up perfectly in Genesis 1:26, where God says: "Let Us make man in Our image, according to Our likeness", where 'Us' and 'Our' refers to the Father, the Son and the Holy Spirit.

THE TRINITY AND THE SUN

The Holy Trinity is one of those concepts which is really hard to grasp, but let's use an analogy to help us out a little. The Sun sits up in the sky, shining light upon the earth, and at the same time bringing forth heat. God the Father exists in heaven, just like the Sun sits in the sky. God the Son came down upon earth and was seen by man, just like we see light shining in the earth every single day. The Holy Spirit is the voice of God inside of us, essentially our personal experience of God, and this is like the heat which we cannot see, but rather feel. Therefore, just like the Sun is three in essence, the Holy Trinity is three in essence as well!

IT WAS GOOD

On the first day God said "Let there be light" and there was light (verse 3) and the light was good (verse 4). Note that God only created the light (not darkness), since God does not create anything wicked or evil. Obviously there was darkness to start with because of the absence of light and the

What the Fathers Say

The new creation is realised by the water and the Spirit, in the same way that the world was created, when the spirit of God was hovering over the face of the waters

– St. Augustine

Why Did God Make Man Last?

God created man at the end to crown him as king over the entire creation. In the Gregorian liturgy, we say that God "did not leave us in need of anything". He created everything for our sakes, gave us authority over all things and said "Be fruitful and multiply; fill the earth and subdue it; have dominion over… every living thing that moves on the earth" (verse 28).

People, Places &Things

absence of goodness on the face of the earth. And why does God say "the light was good"? God is not saying this as if He is surprised by the outcome (since He already knew it would be good) but rather He is emphasising that the light is good for its desired purpose.

After creating the morning and the evening and separating the bodies of water from the dry land, in verse 11 God exclaims: "Let the earth bring forth grass, the herb that yields seed, and the fruit tree that yields fruit according to its kind". Notice that God created the trees fully grown. In the same way which God created Adam as a fully grown adult, God did not need to create the seeds but made the tree immediately. God says 'let it happen' and it does! He made the vegetation and the crops before the Sun so that no one can say life is in the Sun and worship the Sun. God creates with no assistance but allows the Sun and the waters to maintain His perfect creation. This shows the greatness of God as a creator and provider, who does not work on human terms, but on His own divine and heavenly terms.

THE SUN AND THE MOON

Then on day 4 of the creation, God creates the Sun to rule by day and the Moon and the stars to rule by night. Until this point in creation, we don't know exactly what one day really meant (probably thousands of years). But from this point on in the Creation, due to the creation of the Sun and Moon,

What the Fathers Say

You have printed Your traits on us! You created us in Your image and according to Your likeness! You made us Your currency; yet Your coins should not remain in darkness. Send the ray of Your wisdom to scatter our darkness, for Your image to shine in us

— Origen

the day became 24 hour periods as we now know them. Pope Shenouda contemplates that the Sun represents Christ and the Moon represents us. On its own, the Moon is not luminous since it only reflects the light of the Sun. In the exact same way, we are not luminous in our own light, but we reflect the light of God in us when we allow Him into our lives.

So far, whenever God created anything, at the end of the day's creation He says 'it was good'. However, on the sixth day, God creates the animals and says 'it was good' (verse 25) and then creates man and says 'it was very good' (verse 31). This shows that man is the highest level of creation and as such should be distinguished from everything else. The animals, plants and celestial bodies are all 'good' but man is 'very good'. See how much God values each and every single one of us! Humanity was God's masterpiece and the perfection of His entire creation! If God loves and values each and every one of

REFLECTION

When God created humanity, he made us in His image and called us "very good". How often do I reflect God in my life- am I really a good ambassador for Christ in my day to day life?

us so much, then why do we often belittle and devalue ourselves, thinking of ourselves to be nothing? Instead the opposite is true! When someone came to Pope Shenouda and told him "I am dust", the Pope replied in his wisdom: "You are not dust my son. You are a divine breath coming straight from the mouth of God".

CHAPTER 2

THE CREATION COMPLETED

After six days of creation, God decides to rest on the seventh day. The fathers say that the seventh day does not follow the same formula as the first six days, because the seventh day has started but is still not yet finished. Now why does God rest? This is not because God is tired or weary from His work, but rather the term 'rest' in Hebrew simply means 'to finish and stop before starting something else'. God created everything in six days, and now there is no more creation.

In the New Testament, Christ exclaims: "Come to Me, all you who labour and are heavy laden, and I will give you rest" (Mat 11:28), showing us that when we come to Christ, we don't labour but only find rest in Him. When we give our lives to Christ in continuous prayer, Bible reading and following of the sacraments, we find rest in Him and enjoy the salvation of our souls. Being a Christian is not burdensome and does not mean living a restricted life, rather, it means enjoying the freedom of salvation with the Lord. When I am far from God, slack in my prayers and Bible reading, and easily given to sin, then even simple tasks become burdensome and my life becomes filled with stress and worry. I continue to search for joy elsewhere and I cannot find it! However, when I draw near to God, I receive power from the Holy Spirit and nothing can ever faze me!

Events

CHAPTER 2

GOD'S FINAL MASTERPIECE

In verses 7 and 8, the details of man's creation are discussed. God created man from dust and breathed life into him. This was a simultaneous action. It was not as if God created man at one stage, and then breathed life into him after a certain period of time. Both happened at the same time. Similarly, our church believes that the soul of a baby enters into them at conception. There is no time in a human's life where they have a body without a soul, or a soul without a body, for the soul cannot be defined apart from the flesh. This is why our Orthodox church believes in Baptism and Confirmation from the beginning of any human's life.

Notice that God created man outside the Garden, and then later on placed him inside the Garden (verse 8). The Garden here represents the kingdom of God. This

The Garden of Eden

Much debate has existed for centuries over where the Garden of Eden is actually located some suggest that it was completely destroyed in the floods during the time of Noah, others believe that it is a city of complete ruin and debris, whilst other people believe that it is still standing today! From the information provided to us in this chapter, we can conclude that the Garden was in Mesopotamia - modern day Iraq. Moses describes the Tigris and Euphrates rivers, which seem to make the general location clear. However, if we go to this area today, we will find nothing like a lush paradise. Mesopotamia today is arid and 5,000 years of continuous occupation and farming has made the area less fertile and more barren.

People, Places &Things

What the Fathers Say

God wanted to justify man through submission to the commandment; but, at the same time, He wished for man to stay as a child in his simplicity and loyalty to God

- St. Theophilus of Antioch

is important because in no way could Adam or Eve claim that they had rights to enter the Garden (or the kingdom of God) after their fall. A person who is born in a country cannot be thrown outside a country if they do something wrong. However, someone who has citizenship can have his citizenship revoked and be thrown out if they commit a similar wrong-doing. This is the same with Adam and Eve who were given citizenship rather than birthright to enter into the Garden. Man cannot claim to own the kingdom of God, but rather it is a gift given by the grace of God. Our place in the kingdom of heaven is a gift purchased by the blood of Christ, and we have done nothing of our own goodness to deserve it.

GOOD AND EVIL

After placing man inside the Garden of Eden, God commands man to eat of every single tree except for the 'tree of knowledge of good and evil'. To make this warning even more fearsome, whoever ate of this tree "would surely die" (verse 17). Notice that the tree of knowledge of good and evil was placed in the midst of the garden, very close to the tree of life (verse 9). Why is this the case? Because God is giving us a choice, to pursue life or to pursue death. This way, whenever we are faced with temptations (resembling death), we are reminded to run to Christ (the tree of life) who provides us with the strength to overcome sin.

Now God told Adam, whoever eats of the tree of knowledge of good and evil shall surely die. However, when Adam and Eve ate from the tree, they didn't die! Death in the original meaning meant separation from God, and this is the correct meaning of death. After disobeying God's commandments, Adam and Eve became spiritually dead as they found themselves distanced from God! But after the New Testament and Christ's resurrection, regardless of how much or how great our sins, the church has arranged for us sacraments such as Baptism, Confirmation, Holy Communion and Repentance and Confession so that even if we fall into sin, we may never fall into spiritual death!

EVE IS CREATED

God looks at Adam with compassion and realises that he is alone and without a companion of his equivalent! Observe the mercy, love and generosity of God! So in verse 21, God puts Adam to sleep, takes one of his ribs and creates Eve! God puts Adam to sleep because man cannot perceive God's wonderful acts of creation. Man can observe but not witness the miracles of God. The fathers contemplate that Eve did not come from Adam's head so she would not be superior to him, or from his feet so that she would not be inferior to him. Eve came from Adam's side because man was to be equal with woman and this depicts the ideal Christian marriage, the perfect unity between man and woman with Christ in their midst.

> **What the Fathers Say**
>
> They were both naked, yet spiritually covered, thus there was no cause for shame; as what makes one ashamed is not his body, but the corruption that goes into the body because of sin. That is why entering naked into the font of Baptism is a return to paradise, where man was, in his purity of heart naked, yet not ashamed
>
> – Fr Tadros Malaty

GOD KNOWS EXACTLY WHAT WE NEED

Here it is important for us to realise how much God loves and He knows exactly what is best for us. After making the land, the waters, the plants and all the animals for Adam to enjoy, he found Adam still lacking one thing-company! So what does God do? He creates for him a fellow human to experience life with. This teaches us that God will always provide what we need, and therefore, we should always be content with whatever He has provided us.

There is a nice story about spiritual poverty and being content with anything and everything that God has given us. A woman was at the reception of the Serbian Patriarch's residence to discuss business matters. When she entered the residence, she happened to look at the Patriarch's feet, and was shocked at the sight of his shoes: they were old, had been torn and then repaired. The woman thought: "How shameful for us Serbs, that our Patriarch has to go around in broken shoes; couldn't anyone in all of Serbia give him new shoes?". The Patriarch, knowing her thoughts, said to her joyfully: "Look at what good shoes I have! I found them near the garbage cans when I went to the patriarchate. Someone had thrown them away, but they are real leather. So I stitched them up, polished them, and look, they can still be used a long time". This teaches us to be content with whatever we have, and further teaches us that God is

the true provider and that we can find joy,
comfort and consolation in him alone.

REFLECTION

God knows exactly what we need and exactly when we need it. After all, He is our Father and has inscribed us on the palms of his hand. Why then do we worry, complain and refuse to be content with everything that He has given us?

CHAPTER 3

THE BEGINNING OF THE FALL

Events

CHAPTER 3

We're all familiar with the story of Adam and Eve and how the serpent tempted them to eat of the tree of knowledge of good and evil! But what we often overlook is how humanity's downfall began. Eve's first mistake was that she involved herself in a discussion with the serpent. The serpent simply presented the idea of eating from the tree, and instead of completely refuting the idea, Eve opened herself to the idea of breaking God's commandments by compromising with sin. When Satan tempted Jesus on the mountain (Mat 4: 1-11), Jesus taught us the correct way of dealing with temptation by completely resisting even the thought of sin, instead answering Satan with biblical quotes. In the exact same way, we should completely shut the door on bad thoughts and resist them as soon as they begin to enter our minds. This could be through simply leaving the sinful environment, saying a quick prayer or changing the topic immediately.

After Satan planted the thought in Eve's mind, she "saw that the tree was good for food, pleasant to the eyes, and desirable to make one wise" (verse 6). These are the three things which the devil uses to tempt us today. John warns us in his epistle that three things cause us to be separate from God: "the lust of the flesh, the lust of the eyes and the pride of life" (1 John 2:16). The lust of the flesh refers to that which is 'good for food', the lust of the eyes refers to that which is 'pleasant to the eyes' and the pride of life refers to that which

is 'desirable to make one wise'. Therefore, in order to avoid falling into sin and eventual separation with God, we must overcome all the lustful attacks of the devil and any thought of ego or pride which enters into our hearts.

THE FALL AND CONSEQUENCE OF IMPURITY

Now what are the consequences of the fall? The first consequence is that "the eyes of both of them were opened, and they knew they were naked" (Gen 3:7). They were always naked, but now they knew that they were naked. They allowed Satan to take the first step and implant the thought in their mind, and now Satan is in total control and he defiled everything that was good in them. It's as if he hacked into their system and put a virus inside them which spread and infiltrated. They lost their purity and saw sin and shame in their nakedness because now they are thinking like Satan.

Now here lies an important lesson! It is very important for us as youth living in a sexualised and secular society, to resist the devil from the get go. Whenever the devil presents us with a suggestion of lust, whether this be an unhealthy relationship, a sexualised movie scene or advertisement on the TV or even just a fleeting thought we must cut it off from the onset. That way, I declare my loyalty to the Lord and trample down Satan.

The joy and pleasure provided by sexual temptations and attractions are very temporary and short-lived and always lead to guilt, despair and separation from God. In the book of Revelations, St. John the evangelist even described this particular sin as "sweet as honey in your mouth" but "bitter in your stomach" (Rev 10:10). This means that the consequences of this sin are fatal! There are no two ways. Whoever seeks joy from sexual sins cannot achieve joy from the Lord, for only the "pure in heart can see God" (Mat 5:8). Even St. Anthony the first monk was tempted with lustful pleasures and desires as well. Whenever a temptation would enter his mind he would recite the verse: "Let God arise and let His enemies be scattered. Let them that hate him flee from before His face" (Psalm 68:1).

HIDING FROM GOD?

Another question which comes to mind is why did Adam and Eve hide? This is because they were afraid of God. Love brings us closer to God but fear separates us from God. The love of God brings about good fear which leads to repentance, but bad fear turns us further away from God and instead leads us

The Seed of Woman: the first prophesy?

People, Places &Things

Verse 15 is a prophecy about the relationship between Christ and the devil. According to Old Testament custom, it is the man who has a seed and 'plants' it into the woman to produce offspring. There is no such thing as 'the seed of woman'! However, Christ is the only One born of the 'seed of woman' because no man is involved in His incarnation, which came from the Virgin Mary alone. This is one of the first prophecies in the Bible directing us towards the incarnation of Jesus Christ. (Philippians 2: 15).

to blame others. Even while in a state of sin, Adam and Eve's hearts were hardened and they refused to acknowledge their sin and repent. Eve blamed the serpent and Adam even went as far as to blame God, claiming: 'the woman whom YOU gave to be with me, she gave me of the tree and I ate' (verse 12). Our fear of God should lead us to repentance, rather than despair, blame and regret. Don't let Satan make you so ashamed of your sin that you separate yourself from God completely. Our fear of God should be out of love, which brings forth repentance and the forgiveness of our sins. And even if we feel guilty because of our sins, we should remember that His blood was shed for our sake on the Cross and God has removed from us all the memory of evil entailing death.

THE PUNISHMENT FOR SIN

God now advises the serpent and Adam and Eve of the punishments for their respective sins. Unlike with Adam and Eve, God doesn't ask the serpent any questions but advises it of its punishment. When God questioned Adam and Eve, he was trying to lead them to repentance. However, the serpent did not have the same option to repent because animals do not have an immortal soul. Also, Satan already had his chance and failed. Even though the serpent was used as a tool by the devil, it was still cursed to teach humanity a lesson. God doesn't want us to make excuses for ourselves when we fall into sin. He is teaching us not to allow Satan to use us as his tool for evil.

> ## What the Fathers Say
>
> *Negligence and laziness, and not the devil, are the means to overcome the non-alert... through both the devil is given the opportunity to go far in his evil ways*
>
> *– St. Didymus the blind*

What the Fathers Say

Paradise was given to man, and when he proved not worthy of it, he was driven out. When man stayed out of Paradise and felt insulted, this would lead him to repentance and regaining worthiness to enter again. This actually happened when the Lord exclaimed to the thief on the Cross: 'Assuredly I say to you, today, you will be with Me in Paradise' (Luke 23:43)

– St John Chrysostom

REPENTANCE

God then punishes Adam and Eve individually for their sin, and Adam responds by naming his wife Eve, which means 'the mother of all living'. Instead of being angry with Eve for causing him to sin, Adam chooses to call her 'the mother of all living'! Whilst this seems particularly strange, this indicates the start of Adam's repentance and renewed faith and hope in God. He recalls God's promise that through woman's seed, salvation will come to all mankind. God in turn, observing the sincerity of Adam's repentance, clothes him and his wife immediately with garments of sin to cover their nakedness and erase their shame. This teaches us that as soon as the first small steps of repentance are taken, God's grace will enter our lives and transform us entirely!

Therefore we should not despair or become saddened when we fall into sin. A priest once said in a youth meeting that when we fall, we can get back up to an even higher spiritual level than we were before! This means that I should try to avoid sin at all costs, but if it happens and I do fall into sin, I should arise from my sinful act straight away, admit my sins to the Lord and then turn over a fresh page immediately.

ST MOSES THE STRONG

The perfect example of repentance in our Orthodox Church is St. Moses the Strong. This was a man who was a gang-leader, rapist, thieve and worshipper of the Sun amongst many other sins. One day, he prayed, asking the Sun: "if you are God, let me know and if you are not God, lead me to the true God". Immediately, he heard from someone that the monks in the wilderness of Shiheet knew God, so he girded himself and went to meet St. Macarius in the wilderness. After much discussion, St. Moses decided to be baptised into the Christian faith, and publicly confessed all his evil deeds in the church. During this confession, St. Macarius saw a tablet that was all black, representing the sins of St. Moses. Every time St. Moses would mention a sin, the angel would wipe it off the tablet, till the tablet eventually became completely white! This teaches us that no matter how bad your sin is, God's mercy is greater, and He is willing to forgive us regardless. We just need to take the first step and make a conscious decision to repent.

REFLECTION

How many times in my life am I faced with a choice, to do good, or to do evil? How many times have I chosen to gossip or judge, instead of remaining silent? How many times have I enjoyed the sinful environment, instead of fleeing from sin?

CHAPTER 4

Events

CHAPTER 4

CAIN VS ABEL

After being expelled from the garden, Adam and Eve gave birth to Cain and then Abel. The first thing to notice here is that although Cain is older than Abel, the Bible mentions Abel's profession ahead of Cain to show that God accepted Abel's tending of the sheep more than Cain's tilling of the ground. When Adam was still in the Garden of Eden (when he was closer to God), his responsibility was to oversee the animals (tend the sheep). However, after he was cast out of the Garden, his punishment was to labour and till the ground. Both Cain and Abel knew this, and Abel, who was more spiritual, chose the more heavenly role, whilst Cain chose the more earthly role.

Adam and Eve taught both Cain and Abel how to make offerings as they were taught by God. Remember that after their fall, Adam and Eve covered themselves with fig trees, which was rejected by God. God instead covered them with animal skin, and this was sufficient to cover their nakedness. Abel understood this and did what he considered pleasing to God, providing the best of his animals for the offering. However, Cain was stubborn and chose to make the wrong offering, and even then he refused to offer his best fruit! This teaches us a lesson to offer God only the best of what we have. We should not pray in the last 5 minutes of the day when we are already exhausted or read the Bible in the bus on the way to school (although this is a good start), but we should set a designated time for all spiritual activities and stick to this with discipline. This way, we can develop a relationship with God, and this is definitely in our best interest!

CAIN KILLS ABEL

In verses 6-7, one of the interesting characteristics of God are visible. Even though Cain is at fault and even has the audacity to be angry with God, God in His great mercy still speaks to Cain and reasons with him. This teaches us a lesson so that we can never say God only speaks to the righteous. God cares for Cain equally as much as he cares for Abel, and even warns him that sin 'lies at the door... but you should rule over it' (verse 7). God sees the anger building up inside Cain, and tries to convince him against his evil thoughts and bring him back to the righteous path. God (through the grace of the Holy Spirit) tries to

The Land of Nod

After Cain receives his just punishment from God, he flees to the land of Nod, east of Eden (verse 16). The word "Nod" in Hebrew translates to "getting lost/wandering". Thus, after turning against the commandments of God, naturally, Cain found himself empty and lost as well. This holds an important spiritual lesson for us all - when we disobey God and seek pleasures elsewhere, we too will feel this sense of emptiness and loss - Jesus even said "without Me you can do nothing" (John 15:5). Much of the reason why people are depressed, anxious and lonely is because they are left searching for pleasure and joy, and can never find it. For the Christian, true joy and pleasure comes from being with God alone!

People, Places &Things

Moses was in grief and prayed with his heart, to which God responded: 'Why do you cry to Me' (Exodus 14:15). So also did Hannah, whose voice, although not heard, yet received all that she prayed for, as her heart was crying loud (1 Samuel 1:13). Abel, even when dead, his blood cried with a voice louder than a trumpet

– St. John Chrysostom

sway us from our bad thoughts, but at the end of the day, leaves us our free will. Unchecked anger leads Cain to violence and even murder, and therefore we must learn to control our emotions and evil thoughts as soon as they enter our minds.

Just like he did with Adam, God gives Cain a chance to admit his error and show remorse by asking a question rather than making an accusation. And just like Adam, Cain in his pride is defiant and refuses to confess, instead questioning God: 'Am I my brother's keeper?' (verse 9). Yes we are! As Christians, it is our responsibility to look after our brothers and sisters. If we can't love our brothers who we can see, how can we love God whom we can't see? (1 John 4:20).

CAIN BECOMES CURSED

After refusing to admit his error and repent from his sinful ways, God imposes upon Cain the just punishment for his evil actions. When Adam and Eve sinned, the land (not them) was cursed and Satan was cursed too through the serpent. But now, Cain himself is cursed! He is the first human to receive a curse from the Lord God because he gave himself entirely to Satan to be used as his tool. Since Satan was already cursed, this meant that Cain had to be cursed as well. This applies to us as well! If we give our lives to Satan to be used by him, we will be cursed by God! Notice how what started as one small thought of jealousy and anger, led Cain to murder his brother and receive a curse from God. How dangerous are those thoughts which are uncontrolled and how unsafe is a mind which is without discipline!

CAIN STILL COMPLAINS

God gives Cain one final chance to repent and show some remorse in verses 13 and 14. Astonishingly, however, Cain chooses to complain about his punishment: 'You've cast me out and now I'll be killed by anyone who sees me'. God in His mercy puts a sign on Cain so that anyone who kills him will be punished sevenfold (verse 15). Cain killed but is now refusing to be killed! This paradox is typical of an evil person, their selfishness is such that they are happy to hurt others but won't accept when others hurt them back. We should instead strive to do the exact opposite by loving and respecting even those who hurt us.

FR. BISHOY KAMEL AND THE ORANGES

Whilst Cain is a good example of what not to do in the way we treat others, the opposite end of the scale is Father Bishoy Kamel, an Egyptian priest who was alive not long ago. He used to always walk a particular route from his house to the church, and there was a certain non-Christian boy who lived in one of these houses that he would pass on his way. This boy would always curse at Father Bishoy and mock him from the balcony, even throwing orange peels at him. One day as he was going to church, Father Bishoy noticed

> ## What the Fathers Say
>
> *I wish that we do not despise each other, as this makes us as though we are despising God Himself, who asked us to care for others. When Cain despised his brother, he instantly disregarded God Himself*
>
> *– St John Chrysostom*

that the boy did not appear in the balcony to throw the usual abuse and orange peels at him. After the mass, Father Bishoy went and knocked on his door, only to find out from his mother that the boy was in poor health and lie sick in bed. This holy priest then asked the mother if he could visit the boy in his room. Father Bishoy told him how much he missed seeing him, how he hoped that he would get better soon and even gave him a bag full of oranges as a gift as well! The boy never said a bad word to Father Bishoy again! This is a perfect example of how we should treat our enemies, even if they continue to wrong us and this is ultimately the sign of a good and faithful Christian.

REFLECTION

Is my heart truly filled with love for everyone or is there someone who I hate or despise? If so, am I willing to reconcile with them today and make peace, just as God desires?

CHAPTER 5

Events

CHAPTER 5

FROM GENERATION TO GENERATION

Whilst this chapter may just seem like a bunch of names, if we delve a little deeper, there is still a profound spiritual meaning which can be grasped. For starters, whenever we see any name mentioned in the Bible, we should pray that we too become worthy to have our names in written in the book of life. These people have received the honour from God to be mentioned in the Bible, and we too can remind God of His promise: 'Rejoice that your names are written in heaven' (Luke 10:20).

It's important to notice that in this chapter, there is no more mention of Cain or Abel. It's as if the past has been wiped out clean, and we are starting Adam's family fresh with a new genealogy. In verses 1 and 3, we are reminded that man is created in the 'likeness and image of God'. Seth (Adam's son) is created in the likeness and image of God. It's almost as if creation is restarting here. God is telling us to ignore the horror, anger and killing mentioned in chapter 4 and to make a new start with His perfect creation again. Notice the long-suffering grace of God who, regardless of our actions, continues to prolong His mercy and patience with us!

ENOCH

The genealogy goes as per script until verse 24, which says that: 'Enoch walked with God; and he was not, for God took him'. Enoch followed God his entire life, but when he was

65, he 'walked with God' until he was taken at 365 years old. This means that he walked with God 300 years before he reached a level of spirituality which allowed him to be open to the divine. He was the most righteous of all because he consecrated his entire life to God!

From Enoch we learn an extremely important message. There is a chance for each and every one of us to overcome the corruption of the body, and by living a righteous life, we will be saved. One of Satan's biggest traps is to make us feel as if we have no hope, that we have lost our salvation. But Enoch called upon God and was carried to heaven (without death), meaning that if we too put our hope in God, we will be transported spiritually to heaven.

NEVER LOSE HOPE

There is a nice story in the Paradise of the fathers which teaches us to never lose hope in God. There was a monk who lived an

What the Fathers Say

You, like Enoch, would have pleased the Lord, being found worthy of leaving the world behind. The Spirit has taught Solomon that those who please God are early taken and quickly liberated, lest, by staying longer, they get defiled by the filth of the world. And God took him away, lest evil...

The Two Men who never Died

In the history of mankind, there are only two men who have never died. One, Enoch, has already been mentioned above and in verse 24 of this chapter, we learn that "God took him" up to heaven while still alive. The other is Elijah, who was carried up "by a whirlwind into heaven" in a chariot of fire (2 Kings 2:11). It is believed that both prophets will return onto earth before the second coming of the Lord, preaching the word of God for three and a half years, before they are killed as witnesses to God. This was seen in a vision by St. John the beloved, and is recounted in Revelations 11: 1-14.

People, Places &Things

What the Fathers Say

would change his mind; He was pleasing the Lord, so He loved him and took him from among the wicked (Songs 4:11).

– St. Cyprian

extremely sinful life as a youth, committing fornication, murder and many other sins. After he repented, he entered the monastery and became a father and shepherd to all the monks. Whenever the devil would tempt him with a thought of hopelessness or despair, he would reply to the devil: 'My God is so merciful and is able to wipe away all the sins of my youth'. Meanwhile, whenever the devil would tempt him with a thought of pride, he would reply: 'O my soul have you forgotten all the evil and wicked sins of my youth? Weep over your salvation'. In this manner, neither despair nor pride were able to overcome him and he conquered over the devil.

REFLECTION

Just like all the people mentioned in this chapter had their names written in the book of life, how often do I pray that my name is also written in the book of life. How often do I pray to reach the kingdom of heaven, or to find favour with God? After all, it is written: "But seek first the kingdom of God and His righteousness, and all these things shall be added to you". (Mat 6:33)

CHAPTER 6

THE DECLINE OF MAN

In this chapter we observe the beginning of humanity's downfall and decline. Verses 4 and 5 speak of 'giants on the earth', and these giants are the descendants of Cain who lived savage and violent lives with their entire focus on bodily pleasures. They were gigantic people as a result of their self-indulgent lives (like Goliath), and took for themselves whatever they wanted, including many wives because the more they had, the more powerful they were. When the sons of God started to mingle with these evil men, they too left the worship of God behind and began to focus entirely on their physical needs and pleasures as well. They became gigantic and savage so that they could fit in with Cain's people, and this indicated the downfall of man.

God makes a rather peculiar statement in verse 3: 'My Spirit shall not strive with man forever, for he is indeed flesh; yet his days shall be one hundred and twenty years'. This Spirit refers to the Holy Spirit, which guides and leads humanity to repentance. When God saw how lustful and carnal man had become, He still gave them time to repent. It is believed that Noah was preaching repentance for 120 years, and during that time the Holy Spirit was working inside people to bring them to repentance. However, the entire population (except Noah's family) refused the work of the Holy Spirit, and were left to the evil thoughts of their hearts. God gave the people

Events

CHAPTER 6

a time limit to repent, teaching us that we cannot do evil for as long as we like. There is a limit to how long the Holy Spirit will guide us, even if this limit is the day we physically die. Therefore, we should live a life of continual repentance because we can never know the day in which our earthly lives will end and we will face judgement.

GOD'S REGRET?

God is even sorry about His decision to create man, being extremely grieved in His heart (verse 6). Note that God does not regret His decision to make man, because God's decisions do not change. It's not as if He does not know what is going to happen, because God knew that humanity would fall into temptation and lust. Rather than changing His mind, God is using language that we can understand. This verse is an expression of His love and care towards us. It is the wounded spirit of the artist whose work has been rejected; the broken heart of a lover whose love has been rejected.

THE ARK AS THE CROSS

Amidst all the turmoil and corruption that existed within humanity, one righteous man, Noah, still remained. Noah found grace in the eyes of the Lord, and therefore was entrusted with the salvation which came through the Ark. In the wood of the Ark, we see the wood of the Cross. As there was water, so we have the water of baptism. The Ark was a symbol of salvation because all who were in it were

What the Fathers Say

Now, while you are alive, do not delay your repentance. There are many people in Hades right now, who wish for one minute, or one second of your life, to offer repentance, but cannot find it. Your life is a precious blessing from the Lord, repent, whilst you have the opportunity to do so.

— Pope Shenouda III

saved, just like all who come to the Cross are saved. God loves man (even when he's at his worst), and will always look for a means to save us.

THE RIGHTEOUS NOAH

Noah kept God's commandments and remained firm in faith for over 100 years while waiting for the flood. He waited and preached for over 100 years, and won no one (except his immediate family), yet he never lost faith or waivered. Not only that, but he was mocked and humiliated for believing in such a strange concept as a flood (people had never seen rain to this point). He never questioned God, but rather trusted Him entirely even though he saw no immediate fruits for his efforts. This complete, blind faith in the promise of God is what made him such a righteous man. We too should learn to completely place our trust in God, regardless of the circumstances. Remember Jesus' promises: 'look at the birds of the air, for they neither sow nor reap, nor gather into barns, yet your heavenly Father feeds them' and 'Consider the lilies of the

What the Fathers Say

No matter how severe the storm, when you're with God there is always a rainbow waiting at the end

- Fr Tadros Malaty

People, Places &Things

Noah's Ark

God told Noah to build an Ark that would be big enough to save his family and animals that would not otherwise be able to survive a worldwide flood. The ship was to be 300 cubits long by 50 cubits wide by 30 cubits high (Genesis 6:15). In modern day terminology, that means the Ark was 140 metres long, 25 metres wide and 15 metres high! More intriguingly, even scientific evidence supports the existence of Noah's ark! Using underwater robot vehicles, marine archaeologists found evidence of people who perished in a great flood of the Black Sea 7000 years ago, and this has been linked with story of Noah's ark.

field, how they grow: they neither toil nor spin; and yet I say to you that even Solomon in all his glory was not arrayed like one of these' (Mat 6: 25-30).

In verse 13, God takes the time to explain to Noah why He is taking action against mankind. This is because God likes to reveal His plans and mysteries to those who love Him and completely trust Him with all their hearts. When we are still beginners in our spiritual lives, we speak with God and ask for repentance, but for those who became saintly, God reveals His secrets to them. God explains His plans before asking them to do something for Him! This is written in Psalm 25:14 – "The secret of the Lord is with those who fear Him, And He will show them His covenant".

REFLECTION

How easy is it for us to lose hope or faith in God when something goes wrong in life? And how easy would it have been for Noah to lose hope or doubt God during the 100 year process of building the ark? Let us learn from Noah's blind obedience and faith, and whenever we find ourselves doubting God, let us ask God for the gift of this faith!

CHAPTER 7

GENESIS FOR TEENS

Events

THE GREAT FLOOD

In verse 1, the Lord says to Noah: 'Come into the ark, you and all your household'. Notice that God says 'Come into the ark' rather than 'Go into the ark'. This distinction is important because 'Come' implies that God is inside the ark, asking Noah to come to Him. 'Go' could mean that God is outside. God is therefore encouraging Noah and giving him peace and comfort, reassuring him of His support. It is as if God is saying that there will be trials and tribulations but do not fear, because I will be with you throughout the whole journey. Just like the three young men in the furnace (Daniel 3), Daniel in the lion's den (Daniel 6) and Joseph in the pit (Genesis 37) amongst many other examples. God never leaves those who trust Him and obey Him with all their hearts.

Some people may question how Noah funded this massive project of building the ark. The fathers say Noah was a wealthy and distinguished man who was happy to use his wealth to complete this divine work. He put his wealth into something he hadn't seen (it never ever rained on the earth prior to the flood) and he did this for 100 years without giving up. This unwavering faith is what made Noah so righteous and worthy to be saved from the flood.

Just like Noah, there are several modern day examples of famous and wealthy people who used their success and wealth for the glory of God. A famous example of this is Novak Djokovic, a Serbian tennis player who has won over 70 trophies and earned hundreds of millions of dollars over the course of his career. Despite this, Djokovic has repeatedly said: "before I am an athlete, I am an Orthodox Christian". He has also used these riches to build schools in his native country and restaurants made specifically to feed the homeless and crosses himself regularly at the end of his matches. This shows us, that regardless of whatever success or riches we have on earth, we should remember to attribute it to God and use it for God's glory, because He is the provider of all good things.

40 DAYS OF RAIN

Now why does the rain remain on earth for 40 days and 40 nights specifically? Because four resembles the four corners of the earth, and ten is a number of complete perfection. 40 has come to represent the span of man's life on the earth. Christ was in the wilderness for 40 days, the Israelites wandered in the desert for 40 days and both Moses and Elijah fasted for 40 days at a time. Forty resembles a time of renewal. And why did the flood occur specifically after 7 days? This is to remind us of the creation. God is making a new creation by getting rid of all the evil on earth and starting afresh once again.

> **What the Fathers Say**
>
> While the world was mocking Noah, he was torn with grief for his brother's sake, yearning to take them all into the ark to be saved
>
> – Fr. Tadros Malaty

THE ARK IS SHUT

After Noah's family and all the animals enter into the ark, 'the Lord shut' Noah into the ark (verse 16). Why does the Lord shut Noah in the ark, rather than allowing Noah to shut the door for himself? God closed the door from outside, indicating that only God declares who can be saved and who can't. God is the one with the key. It is He who allowed Noah and his family in the ark and it is He who allows us to enter into heaven. Another reason why God doesn't allow Noah to shut the door is so that he can't open it. God doesn't want Noah to have the agony of seeing people dying. Noah is shut in and cannot see the devastation of what is about to take place.

In verses 18-20, the phrase 'the waters prevailed' is repeated three times. This emphasises a 'new creation' taking place by the Trinity. We are being taken back to Genesis 1, because there is a new beginning for the earth. Recall in Genesis 1; the waters covered

What the Fathers Say

Can you put your hope in the world? Whom has it not deceived? To whom has it not lied? It promises much, but gives vert little. Only those who hope in the Lord God can be saved

— St. Anthony of Optina

People, Places &Things

<u>Noah's Ark in our life today?</u>

Even though the story of Noah and the ark is one which occurred thousands of years ago, the relevance is still paramount, even in our day and age now. Noah and his family represent us, the children of God, who find our safety and comfort in the ark, the church of Christ. The waters around the ark resemble the trials and tribulations which face us as believers, and symbolise the temptations which the devil brings our way. Yet we find our safety and comfort in our dwelling with God, and if we remain in His presence, we will never be shaken. In the words of David the psalmist: "Those who trust in the Lord are like Mount Zion, which can never be moved" (Ps 125:1).

the face of the earth, God separated the waters and then the land started to appear. So in Genesis 7, it's like we are going back to the first three days of creation. And just like the earth brought forth all living creatures in Genesis 1, we have the same when the ark is opened and all the creatures come forth from the ark in Genesis 7. And just like the Spirit of God hovered over the waters during the first creation, God likewise blows a wind over the earth (Genesis 8:1) to subsidise the waters. It is as if the process of creation had taken place once again, and this time God removed all corruption from the earth and gave us a second chance.

REFLECTION

Let us learn from the generous heart of Noah- who not only tolerated the criticism of man, but also gave up his possessions and wealth for the sake of God!

CHAPTER 8

Events

CHAPTER 8

THE FLOOD RECEDES

This chapter is basically a continuation of chapter 7. Whilst chapter 7 covers the entry into the Ark and the forty days of rain and flood, chapter 8 continues with the story once the rain stops. Verse 1 says that 'God remembered Noah... and the waters subsided'. This does not mean that God had ever forgotten Noah, but the Hebrew translation simply implies that God is bringing our attention back to Noah. God never neglects or forgets about his children, but always gives them good things in due time. But where could God possibly be in the midst of such a catastrophic and tumultuous flood? God was always present during the flood, but just waited for the right time to intervene. Just like a father who chastens and disciplines his children, God puts us through trials and tribulations only as much as we can handle. And just like God intervened with Noah after so many years, God promises to assist and support us in the due time.

SOME MORE SYMBOLISM

Some of the fathers contemplate on the wind which was made 'to pass over the earth' (verse 1), and this is symbolic of the Holy Spirit who is present during Baptism and Confirmation. So after God baptised the earth (the Ark), He confirmed them in faith by sending the Holy Spirit upon them. Similarly, just like Christ came out of the Jordan River after baptism, the Holy Spirit came upon Him in the form of a dove.

The wood of the ark also resembles the wood of the Cross. The water subsidising took with it all the dead bodies and animals, and only the Ark remained resting on the top of the mountain. There was no more sin or corruption left in the world. This is exactly like the Cross of Christ, which gave us victory over sin and temptation. The sign of the Cross is a powerful weapon against the attacks of the devil, and is guaranteed to give us victory over the devil and all his attacks. The sign of the Cross (like the Ark), is the power given to us by God to trample down all things evil.

EXITING THE ARK

In verses 8-13, Noah sent the dove out three times. The 1st time she came back with nothing. The 2nd time she came back with an olive leaf. The 3rd time she didn't return. Why three times? This is linked to the New Testament. Christ sent the twelve disciples to preach and they came back the first time

What the Fathers Say

If God has shut Noah in, yet He will never forget him amid the waters, but, like a Potter who watches over a clay pot inside the furnace, to take it out in due time as a pot of dignity

— Fr Tadros Malaty

Mountain of Ararat

In verse 4, the ark of Noah lands on the mountains of Ararat. This is believed to be the ark's final resting place, and is located in modern day Turkey. However, despite many vast and expansive search expeditions ranging over thousands of years, there is no concrete evidence which has firmly located any living remnants of the ark today.

People, Places &Things

with no fruit. Then, Christ sent the seventy apostles to preach and they came back to Christ rejoicing from the fruit of their labour (they were able to heal people and cast out demons). The third time, after Christ's resurrection, He sent out the disciples and apostles to preach and they didn't come back to Him because He ascended to heaven.

Therefore, the dove resembles the work of the Holy Spirit in our lives and also signifies our responsibility to preach to others. This preaching does not have to be speaking to people about Christ (although this is certainly good!), but even small things liking giving a friend a cup of water can be considered a means of preaching (Mat 10: 42). And even if people ignore or reject our belief the first or second time, we should not lose hope. Noah spent 100 years warning the people to repent, and not a single soul listened to him! Eventually, however, he became a father to all mankind and God used him as an instrument by which humanity was saved.

NOAH'S THANKSGIVING

Noah's righteousness and faithfulness is demonstrated once again as soon as he exits the ark. Rather than resting or enjoying himself after forty tiresome days in the ark, his first action was to build an altar to the Lord. This is the first mention of 'altar' in the Bible. Previously, they just presented offerings. But this is a new era- to show righteousness by thanking God. We are quick to pray whenever

---

What the Fathers Say

By faith Noah, being divinely warned of things not yet seen, moved with godly fear, prepared an ark for the saving of his household, by which he condemned the world and became heir of the righteousness which is according to faith

– Hebrews 11:7

we need something from God- whether it be to pass an exam or for a sick family member- but we often forget to thank God. Just like God smelt a nice aroma in Noah's sacrifice, He smells the same aroma in our thanksgiving and accepts them.

One of the fathers said that 'there is no gift without increase, except the gift of thanksgiving', teaching us to thank God for absolutely everything and anything he has given us. The church teaches us this important lesson by placing the thanksgiving prayer at the start of all our services in the Agpeya, Liturgy and even in funerals!

REFLECTION

Why do we so often feel that God has abandoned us during various trials and tribulations? Just like in the case of Noah, God is always working, always listening to our prayers, and most importantly, He always has our best interests at His heart!

CHAPTER 9

GENESIS FOR TEENS

GOD'S INSTRUCTIONS TO NOAH

As we have mentioned before, there are several similarities between the story of Noah and the occurrences which took place when God created Adam. God created Adam and Eve to multiply and fill the earth, exactly like God's instructions to Noah in verse 1. Additionally, the authority which God gave Adam over the creation is returned to Noah (verses 2 and 3). When Adam sinned, he lost his authority and dominion over the creation. God now restores this back to Noah as the 'new Adam'. Also, in both cases, there are conditions about what to eat. For Adam, he was instructed to eat from all the trees except the tree of knowledge of good and evil. For Noah, it was to eat of all plants and animals except those with live flesh (i.e. with blood in them). This teaches us that even though God is willing to forgive us time and time again, we must still strive to follow the commandments and live a life which is pleasing to Him. God's continuous forgiveness is not an excuse for us to sin, but rather a motivation for us to avoid falling into sin.

In verses 8-11, God introduces the concept of a 'covenant' (a contract between God and Man). This is a covenant of love because it had no conditions for man. God did not say 'I will no longer flood the earth BUT man has to do such and such…'. God promises not to flood the earth and destroy humanity full stop! There was no disclaimer for God. This comforted Noah, because regardless

Events

CHAPTER 9

of how evil man became again, God would never break his promise. In alike manner, when we make peace with others, we should not impose conditions for our forgiveness and love. When God forgives, He forgives completely and with no partiality. We too, when we forgive, should aspire to do the same. In the Lord's Prayer, the only condition which Jesus imposed upon us is to forgive each other: 'Forgive us our trespasses, as we forgive those who trespass against us'. (Mat 6:12) If we learn to forgive regardless of how

Drinking alcohol: is it a sin?

The topic of drinking alcohol has always been a very controversial issue within Christian communities. Some people argue that the Bible never condemns the consumption of alcohol, only drunkenness. Other people say that even Jesus converted water into wine, whilst others point towards the fact that some other Christian communities permit and do not condemn the consumption of alcohol in a social setting. However, as Orthodox Christians, we are advised strongly against the drinking of alcohol, even within a social setting. Why? Perhaps the most powerful argument against the use of alcohol pertains to health issues. Our bodies are the temple of the Holy Spirit, a gift from God. Alcohol, meanwhile, is a known poison that can cause significant health issues- yes, some people even die from alcohol overdoses! Further, even if people drink without the intention of getting drunk, within a social setting, it is very tempting to have "one more drink" and one often leads to two and three and so on. Therefore, instead of running the risk of getting drunk and all the consequences that comes with it, as Christians focused on the kingdom of heaven, why would we jeopardise ourselves and potentially fall into sin?

People, Places &Things

badly we have been wronged, then we can rest assured that God will forgive us our sins as well.

NOAH BECOMES DRUNK

After 600 years of living a righteous life and following the commandments of God, Noah drinks of wine and becomes drunk. This is a sinful act in itself, and it seems at odds with Noah's holy and righteous character. The fathers explain that this is the first time on record that man had drunk of the fruit of the vine. This means that Noah did not understand the effects of the alcohol on him. There had been no previous record of any drunken behaviour by man- until then the evil in the world stemmed from violence, murder and sexual immorality. So rather than being deliberate, Noah's sin came out of sheer ignorance and inexperience.

It's also important to notice the difference between Ham and his brothers Shem and Japheth. When Ham saw his father naked, he stopped and stared at his father, before ridiculing him in front of his brothers. He could have so easily rectified the situation by covering his father's nakedness, but instead fell into the sin of judgement and even gossiped about his father. Shem and Japheth on the other hand saw their father naked, and immediately covered him (verse 23). Note that Noah being naked was not sinful in itself, for it is believed that Noah had been working in the field and simply retired for some sleep naked. The issue was that Ham walked in on his naked father, and this was inappropriate and unlawful in the context.

When we see our brethren falling into sin, there are two paths which we can take. We can follow the path of Ham by judging, ridiculing, gossiping and humiliating them in front of others. Or we can take the path of Shem and Japheth by excusing them and covering their sins. The more harshly we judge our brothers for their sins, the more harshly God will judge us for our sins. There was a story of a lazy monk who lived in one of the monasteries in Egypt. Whilst the other monks were disciplined in their church attendance, prayer and fasting, this monk preferred to eat and sleep in luxury than follow a strict spiritual rule. On the day of his departure, all the monks in the monastery surrounded him on his deathbed to bid him farewell. Whilst all the monks wept over their dying brother, the lazy monk comforted his brethren. The abbot of the monastery, worried over the salvation of this monk, asked him: 'Father, don't you feel as if you could have struggled a little more in your lifetime? Don't you feel as if you were spiritually slack at times?' The lazy monk smiled confidently and replied: 'Father, it is true that I have not prayed or fasted as much as I should have, but from the moment I entered this monastery, I have not judged a single soul. There is no way that God can judge me'. The abbot, shocked by this response,

What the Fathers Say

"If Noah did wrong by getting drunk and naked, yet God, in His loved, not only covered his weakness, but also turned this weakness to good, as He did when He turned the evil plan of Joseph's brothers against him to his and their good"

– Fr. Tadros Malaty

replied: 'Go your way son, for you have won the kingdom of heaven with no labour'.

REFLECTION

When we see our brothers or sisters falling into sin or making a mistake, how often do we expose and judge them, rather than make for them excuses and covering their sins? If we don't cover the sins of our brethren, then how can we expect God to cover our sins as well?

CHAPTER 10

Events

CHAPTER 10

NATIONS DESCEND FROM NOAH

This is another of those chapters which are just filled with names, emphasising the historical accuracy of the Bible. It is the only ancient document that goes into such detail of both ancient nations and names. Whilst it may not be as interesting or eye-opening as other chapters within the book of Genesis, it contains a complete summary of humanity's ancestry tree. Considering that Noah's family was the only family on the face of the earth after the flood, Noah can be considered a forefather to us and to humanity as a whole.

Verses 1-5 of the genealogy start with the youngest son Japheth. Seven of his sons are mentioned, and likewise seven of his grandsons too. Japheth was the father of the modern day Europeans and his descendants settled in Europe, as well as northern Asia. The sons of Japheth spread to Greece, Cyprus, Turkey, Russia and Persia (modern day Iran) amongst many other countries around the world.

Verses 6-20 cover the sons and grandsons of Ham, Noah's middle child. Ham is considered to be the father of the modern day Middle Eastern and African Nations. His sons and grandsons spread to Egypt, Lebanon, Syria, Iraq, Yemen and their surrounding regions. One of Ham's grandsons, Nimrod, is described to be an extremely controversial figure in the Bible. Verse 9 describes Nimrod as 'a mighty hunter before the Lord', meaning that he was against God. Being a strong and mighty hunter, Nimrod was filled with much arrogance. He believed that his hunting skills meant that he didn't need God because he was able to feed himself. He convinced others to join him in rebellion against God, and this is what lead to the construction of the tower of Babel, which will be discussed in the next chapter. This shows us the consequences that occur when we lack the fear of God.

Verses 21-32 discuss Shem and his sons, grandsons and great grandsons. Now why is Shem mentioned last even though he is the eldest among Noah's three children? It is from Shem which the Israelites, God's chosen people, come into the earth. Since they are God's chosen people, Moses mentions them last to place more emphasis upon them, highlighting their importance in the eyes of God.

What the Fathers Say

I am your father and teacher, all of you my children, listen to my commandments, for I ask you my beloved children, preserve and look after the faith of the Holy Trinity. I ask of you my beloved children, that the fear of God be within you

– Pope Shenouda III

Why was Shem considered to be the blessed one?

In the previous chapter (Gen 9:23), we see that when Noah became drunk and was naked, Shem and Japheth didn't observed their father's nakedness but brought garments to cover him up. Perhaps this is why Noah exclaimed in Gen 9: 26 "Blessed be the Lord, the God of Shem and may Canaan be his servant". Because Shem covered his father's sin, he received blessing from God and from his lineage, the Lord Jesus Christ Himself was born.

People, Places &Things

CHAPTER 11

THE VANITY OF EARTHLY AMBITIONS

Just like the flood in the days of Noah, the story of the Tower of Babel was another significant turning point in the history of mankind. The story here picks up mainly from Ham's family, and in particular Nimrod, the mighty hunter who decided that he didn't need God. He was the one who instigated the concept of a tower that would reach heaven. He wanted to be higher than everyone else and govern over all the people. This reflects humanity's desire for worldly ambitions. Humans reach out for entertainment, wealth, lust and many more things which are beyond our capacity. When these ambitions have no end, inevitably we will lose our faith, fall into rebellion against God and eventually fall into despair.

SOLOMON: VANITY OF VANITIES

A classic example of this from the Old Testament was Solomon. Being chosen by God, Solomon started off in the right path, obeyed the commandments and built the temple according to God's instructions (1 Kings 6: 14). However, his earthly ambitions and desires took complete control over him, and slowly he started straying and losing direction. In his worst state, Solomon had 700 wives and 300 concubines, as well as building for himself vineyards, orchards, gardens and an entire earthly empire. Solomon summed it up perfectly himself when he said: 'whatever my eyes desired, I did not withhold from them'

Events

CHAPTER 11

(Ecclesiastes 2:10). However, at the end of his life, he realised that all these earthly things he desired were 'vanity of vanities and grasping for the wind', a phrase he repeats over thirty times in the book of Ecclesiastes. After spending a whole lifetime pursuing whatever his heart desired, he realised at the end of his life that only God is worth searching for.

THE TOWER OF BABEL

Now why did Nimrod and his followers decide to build a tower to heaven? There are two reasons. Firstly, in their pride, they wanted everyone to look up to them. They thought that they were better than everyone else. Pride is the hardest sin to repent from because it doesn't allow the person to see the error of their ways. The fathers call it the cancer of sins and say it is the hardest to control. The other reason they wanted to build the tower to heaven was because they doubted God's promise of no flood. They foolishly believed the tower would protect them if another flood came. This makes their sin twofold. Not only did they doubt God's

> **What the Fathers Say**
>
> A Christian needs two wings to fly to paradise: humility and love.
>
> – Fr Tadros Malaty

The Tower of Babel

We all know what happened when the tower of Babel was built; God confused the people and they all began to speak in different languages, therefore being unable to communicate with each other. But did you know that the word "Babel" in Aramaic means confusion? Also, before this significant incident in history, there was no such thing as English, Arabic and French. The world only spoke one language- known as the "Adamic language", which is most likely the Hebrew language that is still spoken in Israel today.

> **People, Places &Things**

promise, but they thought that they could outsmart God and reach His level.

In verses 5-9, when God sees the people erring in sin once again, He comes at them with something totally unexpected; they are now speaking different languages! We don't know how God did this, because his methods are incomprehensible to the human mind. All we know is that each family (or nation) could understand each other, but not across different families or nations. Since they could no longer communicate with each other, any potential plans to build the Tower of Babel were now destroyed. Note that God did not do this out of anger or revenge, but rather with the intention to stop the evil which was about to take place.

PRIDE COMES BEFORE THE FALL: NEBUCHADNEZZAR

Perhaps one of the most famous stories regarding pride in the Bible comes directly from the Old Testament from a man called Nebuchadnezzar. This man was a great ruler, blessed with power and riches. He was very well respected in Babylon and beyond and had the gift of abundance, success and riches. His problem? He failed to acknowledge that God was the source of all these gifts. He was so consumed by pride, and exclaimed: "Is not this great Babylon, which I have built for a royal dwelling by my mighty power and for the honour of my majesty?" (Daniel 4: 29). Immediately afterwards, a voice came from

What the Fathers Say

Better is the person who has sinned, if he knows he has sinned and repents, than the person who has not sinned and thinks himself righteous.

– The Desert Fathers

heaven saying "King Nebuchadnezzar, the kingdom has departed from you! And they shall drive you from men, and your dwelling shall be with the beasts of the field. They shall make you eat grass like oxen" (Daniel 4: 31-32). These words were immediately fulfilled, and this former king became like the beasts of the field, walking on four limbs like the animals, with his hair like eagles' feathers and his nails like birds' claws (Dan 4: 33). Not only did he lose his kingdom, power and authority, but he became like a wild beast, and was scorned and ridiculed by all men. Only after he repented and realised his the error of his ways, did God restore him to his original humanity and authority!

REFLECTION

Why are we always so diligent in seeking after worldly success, - whether this be a job, a relationship or any other materialistic thing? Don't we realise that this is all "vanity of vanities", and that there will be a time very soon when this all perishes. Instead, let us remember to seek God first (Matt 6:33). He is the provider of all these things, and knows what we want and need even before we ask!

CHAPTER 12

ABRAM: CALLED BY GOD

This chapter marks the start of the family which is to become God's chosen people. Just like Noah was chosen from amongst the evil around him, Abram was also chosen from the evil which began to appear again. This shows the mercy of our loving God even if there is only one righteous person, God will make the effort to save him and save the entire world. Just like God made a covenant with Noah and with Abram, we too are called by God as His chosen people. We have been given the grace of the knowledge of Christ, and it is our responsibility to remain loyal to God until our last breath.

In verse 1, God instructs Abram to leave three things behind: his country, his family and his father's house. We too, if we desire to follow Christ, must forsake all our desires, our sins and anyone who causes us to stray from Him. The greatest commandment is to love God from all our heart, our mind and our intentions (Mark 12: 30). This means that no earthly ambition or desire should come in the way of our relationship with God. We should remember Christ's instructions to 'Seek first the kingdom of God and its riches, and all these things shall be added to you' (Mat 6: 33). And even though God asked Abram to forsake these three things, God promised him six things in return. These are: 1. Make him a great nation, 2. Bless him, 3. Make his name great, 4. Bless those who bless him, 5. Curse those who curse him, 6. In Abram, all the

Events

CHAPTER 12

families of the earth will be blessed (verses 2-3). God doesn't take without giving back a lot more than what he took, demonstrating to us His generosity and kindness.

A classic example of this is the story of St. Anthony the Great. His father was a noble and rich king, a man with many possessions- a beautiful wife, happy children and male and female servants amongst many others. He lived a good and noble life, but after his death, his memory was erased from the earth as he rested in his grave. Seeing the vain and passing nature of this world and observing his dead father's body, St. Anthony then went to church one day and heard the words of Christ in the gospel: "if you want to be perfect, go, sell what you have give to the poor and you will have treasure in heaven" (Mat 19: 21). He then immediately decided that he would forsake the world of his own will, and seek only the kingdom of God. And not only did he win the kingdom of heaven for himself, but he

What the Fathers Say

Would that I O Lord, forget all things on this world, and You alone should remain to satisfy my life

- Pope Shenouda III

The Lord said to Abram?

We tend to notice a common trend throughout the Old Testament- God speaking to His chosen people. In this chapter, verse 1 says that "the Lord said to Abram" and again in verse 7 "the Lord appeared to Abram". But how and why does God appear to His children so often in the Old Testament? Perhaps the reason why God appeared so much in the Old Testament was because they didn't have the word of God (the Bible) to guide them, nor the Sacrament (such as Baptism and Holy Communion) for God to dwell inside of them. And how does God appear in the Old Testament? Was He an angel? A man? We don't know. All that we do know is that this was Theophany (appearance) of the Son, because whenever God physically manifests Himself to people, this is always in the form of the Son.

People, Places &Things

became a father to thousands of monks, and his memory remains in our church forever.

MORE TRIALS AND TRIBULATIONS

In verse 10, Abram went to Egypt because a famine had come on the land. After every spiritual revival, there always seems to be a trial or tribulation around the corner. Verses 1-9 demonstrated how great Abram was. He was chosen by God, he built altars and preached the word to all people. The following verse however, shows Abram hitting a major road block. God allows for these trials and tribulations to aid us in our spiritual growth. Even Christ, immediately after His baptism, was led by the Spirit into the wilderness for temptation. This teaches us that we too should anticipate and expect a similar fate whenever we begin to spiritually progress.

DID ABRAM LIE?

Whilst some would argue that Abram's first mistake was lying to Pharaoh about the identity of Sarai, even before this he had already committed wrong. He fled from Canaan (the land which God had instructed him to dwell in), without consulting or seeking God. He took matters into his own hands and made the decision completely for himself. Note that Abram was still a good person because he didn't run back to his old land and abandon God completely. His faith in God prevented him from doing this, but his weakness led him to make the decision

What the Fathers Say

Whoever you may be, always have God before your eyes; whatever you do, do it according to the testimony of the Holy Scriptures; in whatever place you live, do not easily leave it. Keep these three precepts and you will be saved

– St Anthony the Great

without first consulting God. We must learn from this that before every decision we make in our life, we must consult God in prayer and seek the guidance of our elders/fathers of confession.

As Abram was about to enter Egypt, he faced another dilemma. He observed the beauty of this wife Sarai, and in fear over his own life, asked her to lie and say that she is his sister instead of his wife. Was this correct? Certainly not! Abram displayed weakness in that he forgot that God could have helped him regardless of the situation. He put his trust in deception rather than in His God. But even though Abram displayed weakness, God is not weak and delivered Sarai from the hands of Pharaoh. Notice how even if we fall into weakness, God is still willing to protect and deliver us regardless of the situation! However, we should always learn to trust in God's divine ability to protect and cover for us, and never forget in His all powerful abilities

REFLECTION

How often do we face trials and tribulations and immediately begin to question God? Even Abram, who followed God's commandments and made sacrifice after sacrifice, faced several hardships throughout his life. Let us learn to accept these hardships, knowing that God permits all things for our growth and spiritual benefit!

CHAPTER 13

ABRAM FLEES FROM EGYPT

Immediately after God delivered Abram from murder and Sarai from the hands of Pharaoh, Abram fled from Egypt. The Bible says that Abram 'went up' from Egypt- arising up from his spiritual weakness. Whenever we are in a state of spiritual weakness, God never leaves us but encourages us to 'rise up' again. It's ok to fall spiritually every now and then, but is extremely dangerous to stay down and delay our repentance. The right attitude to have is 'when I fall, I will arise' (Micah 7:8).

FALLING AND RISING UP AGAIN

After one of his weekly sermons, a man complained to Pope Shenouda, claiming that 'every time I repent, I fall again. So why should I even repent in the first place?'. Pope Shenouda smiled at the man with sympathy and told him: 'Instead of saying "every time I repent, I fall", maybe you should say "every time I fall, I repent" and be more positive about your spiritual life'. This simple lesson teaches us that regardless of how many times we fall, God is willing to forgive us as long as we are willing to forgive ourselves and offer repentance. Therefore even if we fall one hundred times, we must rise one hundred times and God will accept us. However, this does not mean that we use and abuse God's mercy, rather, every time we fall, we must rise with the intention of changing and not falling into the same sin again.

Events

CHAPTER 13

ABRAM VS LOT

After fleeing from Egypt, some tension arises between Abram and Lot. Whilst this strife started off between their herdsmen (verse 7), eventually it escalated to a division between Abram and Lot. As per tradition, Abram was the elder of the two and therefore should have been given the choice of land. However, Lot showed no respect by not only choosing where to live, but also looking for the best land for himself. Lot preferred his own selfish ambition over respect for his uncle Abram, and therefore was totally in the wrong.

However, Lot's sin was not only limited to a lack of respect for his eldest, or selfish ambition. To make matters worse, Lot chose the land knowing that it was full of sin and wickedness! (verse 13) He was so blinded by materialistic desires that he didn't care

What the Fathers Say

When you die, God will not ask you why you sinned, He will ask you why you have not repented

– Pope Shenouda III

Always getting what you want

As mentioned above, Lot sought after physical wealth and riches, whilst Abram sought that which was divine and pleasing to the heart of God. Now many people believe that you can't always get what you want in life. There are things that we want, even demand, that we know we will never get. But Biblically speaking, you can always get what you want. What do I mean? Well, if your heart is aligned with God's heart, when He is enough for you, you only want what He wants to give you. Of course, we will pray and ask for certain things, but whatever He gives us is more than enough. Then we can say with David the psalmist: "Whom have I in heaven but you? And there is nothing on earth that I desire besides you" (Ps 73: 25). This is what Abram understood and applied in his conflict with Lot.

People, Places &Things

What the Fathers Say

If you fall into sin, stand up! When a child falls, what does he do? He raises his hand to his mother or father to help him up," the Pope said. "Raise your hand and God will help you; this is the dignity of God's forgiveness.

— Pope Shenouda III

about what evil was in the Jordan Plain. We should strive to learn from Lot's mistakes and instead consult with our elders, not be driven by materialistic desires and be aware of the company which we keep. It is later reported that Lot 'tormented his righteous soul from day to day by seeing and hearing their lawless deeds' (2 Peter 2: 6-8), illustrating the danger of keeping evil company.

ABRAM THE PEACEMAKER

Abram on the other hand, chose to keep peace between him and Lot. This was not a sign of weakness, but rather a testament to his peaceful and generous soul. Even though he had every right to choose the land he wanted, he resolved the conflict by compromising his position and compromising his rights. Trying to resolve conflicts by giving up our rights seems to be extremely dangerous. It would be, if we left God out of the equation. But Abram made himself vulnerable and trusted in God, and therefore received his reward. God rewarded him with the whole land- the north, south, east and west, and in turn Lot suffered in the land of Sodom and Gomorrah.

This teaches us that when we make sacrifices for others, God will reward us in abundance- either on earth, but most importantly and definitely in the kingdom of heaven. Jesus said in His sermon on the mount: "Blessed are the peacemakers, for they shall be called sons of God" (Mat 5: 9), and by keeping the peace between himself and Lot, Abram truly deserved to be called a son of God.

REFLECTION

When we fall into sin, how often do we feel disheartened and helpless? The devil's greatest trick is to force us into despair and believing that we are too evil to be saved. However, God's mercies are new every morning (Lam 3:22-23) and as far as the east is from the west (Psa 103:12), He has separated our sins from us! Let us run to God whenever we sin, trusting in His infinite compassion and forgiveness.

CHAPTER 14

     GENESIS FOR TEENS

THE TOXIC NATURE OF SIN

Not only was Lot exposed to sin in Sodom and Gomorrah, his next tribulation was even greater than the first. He was also taken away captive by the king, adding insult to the injury of living within such a sinful environment! Observe how Lot's selfish ambition led him to keep company with evil people, which in turn led him to suffer captivity within his own city. This is the nature of sin. One small sin leads to another greater sin, leading to a vicious cycle with both earthly consequences and punishment on the day of judgement (unless we repent and confess).

ABRAM FORGIVES AND SAVES LOT

Seeing Lot's adversity, Abram has compassion upon him, going out of his way to deliver him from the hands of his captives. Even though Lot had sinned against Abram, Abram was happy to risk his life for the sake of his nephew. Instead of holding a grudge against Lot (which would have been completely understandable), Abram completely forgives Lot for his sin. How many of us would do the same? It could have been so easy for Abram to say 'Let him deal with it himself' or 'He deserves it', but in an act of complete kindness and forgiveness, he overlooks his nephew's iniquity and choses to deliver him from the evil which he is about to face. Lot rebelled against Abram, disrespecting him and selfishly choosing the

Events

CHAPTER 14

good land for himself, yet Abram overlooks all this in love and mercy.

How great is the beauty of forgiveness? For the Lord Jesus Himself promised forgiveness to those who also forgive others! (Mat 6:12) Very recently, a story made the news about a drunk driver who ran over and killed four young children (including three siblings) on a footpath in Sydney. News reporters interviewed Leila Abdallah, the mother of the three siblings who were killed, and remarkably, she said: "Right now I can't hate him. I think in my heart I forgive him. I'm not going to hate him, because that's not who we are". How remarkable and unbelievable that the mother of children who were killed

What the Fathers Say

Poor people are the ones who will transport our luggage to heaven

– St John Chrysostom

People, Places &Things

The Three Hundred and Eighteen Soldiers

In verse 18, Abram sends three hundred and eighteen fighters to defeat the evil kings and save Lot. But how could these mere servants defeat such a great army? These servants were born in Abram's house, a house built on faith. This teaches us the importance of having strong faith and a solid understanding of our core Orthodox beliefs. Without this firm faith, we will not stand a chance against the attacks of the adversary. Only those with faith can win the war against evil. Some of the fathers liken these three hundred and eighteen fighters to the three hundred and eighteen bishops assembled at the council of Nicaea (325A D). As these fighters overcame such insurmountable odds, so too did these bishops defeat the arguments of many heretics who denied that the God the Father and God the Son are one in essence and preserved the faith of the church. With the guidance of St. Athanasius, they preserved the Christian faith, and wrote the Nicene Creed, which Orthodox churches recite in every service and liturgy.

would forgive the man who killed them! This is a sign of true and perfect Christianity after Jesus' own heart.

ABRAM MEETS MELCHIZEDEK

In verse 18, Melchizedek is mentioned as the first priest in the Bible. His name comes from the Hebrew words 'melchi' (king) and 'zedek' (sedeek- righteous), meaning the Righteous King. Melchizedek is a representative of Christ, and even offers bread and wine which is symbolic of the body and blood of Christ. This is a prophecy of the priesthood of Christ, which is emphasised in Psalm 110:4: 'You are a priest forever according to the order of Melchizedek'. Notice that Melchizedek gave Abram the bread and wine after he won the war. We too, should partake of the Eucharist once we have conquered sin by faith and the grace of Christ. Partaking of the Body and Blood of Christ is not something which we should take for granted. Even St. Paul warned the Corinthians that 'whoever eats and drinks of this Body and Blood in an unworthy manner eats and drinks judgement to himself' (1 Cor 11:27). However, we must remember that partaking of the Body and Blood of Christ itself gives us strength and power to overcome sin- therefore, we must partake of the Eucharist regularly and with seriousness to advance in our spiritual lives.

GIVING TITHES

Finally Abram gave Melchizedek tithes. This is the first time in which tithes are

What the Fathers Say

The Eucharist is a fire that inflames us, that, like lions breathing fire, we may retire from the altar being made terrible to the devil.

– St. John Chrysostom

mentioned in the Bible, and has become a biblical commandment practiced even till this day. In both the Old and New Testament, the act of almsgiving is of significant importance. There is a nice story in the Paradise of the Fathers of a monk who lived a life of complete poverty. One day, a visitor came to this poor monk's cell to take a blessing. Wanting to provide this man with a gift, the poor monk looked around his cell and found nothing but his Bible. After hesitating for an instant, he offered this man the Bible as a gift and said: 'I have given away the book which told me to sell everything I have and give to the poor'. The man left happy and the poor monk received many blessings for this extreme act of kindness.

REFLECTION

Why are we always so diligent in seeking after worldly success, - whether this be a job, a relationship or any other materialistic thing? Don't we realise that this is all "vanity of vanities", and that there will be a time very soon when this all perishes. Instead, let us remember to seek God first (Matt 6:33). He is the provider of all these things, and knows what we want and need even before we ask!

CHAPTER 15

ABRAM SEES GOD

After delivering his nephew Lot and defeating the enemy, God wants to reward Abram for his good work and appears to him in a vision- not a word or a dream. Whilst a word is to hear a voice and a dream is to see things while asleep, a vision is to see things while awake, and this is the highest level of communication with God. The fathers believe that God the Son appeared to Abram, and this is confirmed when He says 'I AM (the Son) your shield' (verse 1). Furthermore, in verse 5, God 'brought Abram outside', establishing that this apparition was that of God the Son, rather than the Father or the Holy Spirit.

ABRAM'S PRAYER

Abram then complains to God about being childless. However, rather than asking or demanding God to give him a son, he simply states: 'Look you have given me no offspring' (verse 3). He states his problem and does not impose upon God a solution. This is the ideal type of prayer, and is most acceptable to God. When the Son was praying in the Garden of Gethsemane he cried: "Father, if it is Your will, take this cup away from Me; nevertheless, not My will, but Yours, be done." (Lk 22: 42). This is how our prayers should be- we should tell God our problem, and then trust that He will figure everything out in due time. By trusting and submitting to God's will in 100% faith and confidence, we will never be anxious or worried for anything. Instead, we will follow the commandments of God: "Be anxious for nothing, but in everything by prayer and supplication, with thanksgiving, let your requests be made known to God and the peace of God , which surpasses all understanding, will guard your hearts and minds through Christ Jesus" (Phil 4: 6-7).

Notice how once God promises Abram that his descendants will be like the stars of the sky, Abram believes Him straight away (verse 6). He does not for a second doubt the word of God, but accepted his word in complete faith. Abram believed the promise in Genesis 12:1, and he continued to believe it in this chapter as well. This shows that Abram's faith was living and growing, something dynamic. Abram's relationship with God was not static, but rather progressed day by day. We should

What the Fathers Say

Know and remember always, that whatsoever hurts will be dulled as soon as you learn in all things to look at Me. Everything has been sent to you by Me, for the perfection of your soul. All these things were from Me

— St. Seraphim of Viritsa

"Do not be afraid" in the Bible

The words "Do not be afraid" have been used time after time in the Bible, coming straight from the mouth of God. From Christ's final sermon on the Mount to the time when Archangel Gabriel appeared to St. Mary, and also when God appeared to Moses, the message has been the same for generations. In fact, "do not be afraid" was repeated 365 times in the Bible. That's once for every day in the year! The first person in the Bible to receive this message was Abram. God told Him: "Do not be afraid. I am your shield" (verse 1). Notice how Abram offered his life and possessions for the sake of his nephew, and therefore enjoyed the Lord Himself as His shield. As he rejected the earthly reward of possessions and riches, He received the Word of God Himself as a reward. By keeping peace and forgiving Lot, he received a message of peace from the Most High Himself. Therefore, let us approach God, not only in prayer, but also in service to our brethren. In this way, we too can hear the words: Do not be afraid. I am your shield" (verse 1).

People, Places &Things

What the Fathers Say

For God, there are no difficult problems and no difficult solutions. To God, everything is simple. He does not use a greater power for the supernatural things and a lesser power for the natural things. He uses the same power for everything. The most important thing is to cling to God

— St. Paisios of Mt Athos

aspire to be the same in our spiritual lives. With the guidance of our confession fathers, we should aim to increase our prayers and Bible readings to grow and prosper even further in our spiritual lives. In turn, God sees that we put in genuine and heartfelt effort, and begins to give us strength to overcome sin and grow closer in a relationship with Him

A PROPHECY OF THE CROSS

After forming the covenant with Abram, God instructs him to prepare an offering. However, this was not any normal offering. God asked Abram to bring him 3 animals and 2 birds, cut them lengthwise, and place the two halves on top of each other in a perpendicular fashion. Why so much detail? Because this was in the shape of the Cross, pointing towards the ultimate sacrifice of Christ.

Everything in the Old Testament has a link to the New Testament. In Genesis 1, the three essences of the Holy Trinity are present, and this is also the case in John 1. In Genesis 6, the ark of Noah resembles the Cross of Christ whilst the water of the flood represents the water of Baptism. In Genesis 14, the High Priest Melchizedek paves the way for Jesus Christ Himself. And in Genesis 15, Abram's offering is another symbol of the Cross. The Old Testament as a whole is filled with many prophecies and symbolism which ultimately emphasise the accuracy of the Bible from both a spiritual and historical perspective. The unity between the Old and New Testament is one of the greatest proofs highlighting the absolute truth of the Bible.

REFLECTION

When we pray, how often do we impose our will upon God when making requests? Let us learn to leave all matters in God's hands and pray that God's will be done alone, and that this will be sufficient for us! After all, He is our Father and knows what is best for us even before we ask.

CHAPTER 16

SARAI VS HAGAR

So far in Genesis, we have already seen the rivalry between Cain and Abel, as well as that of Abram and Lot. In this chapter, another rivalry arises, but this time between Sarai (Abram's wife) and Hagar (Sarai's maidservant). But before we delve deeper into this chapter, it is important to consider the context of the time. In the olden days, any childless couple was considered to be 'cursed' and the woman was considered to be 'barren'. Additionally, at the time it was considered acceptable to have concubines because there was no written law about marriage (meaning that Abram did not sin by sleeping with Hagar).

The main focus in the chapter is Sarai. It's been over ten years since God has promised Abram a child, and so far none of God's promises have come to fruition. Sarai decides to take matters into her own hands, and asks Hagar (her mistress) to lie with Abram in order to conceive a child. This is an obvious mistake from Sarai, who displayed little faith in God. Here lies an important lesson for us all. Instead of forcing matters with our own hands, we should wait on the Lord. In the New Testament, God states that: 'He who promises is faithful' (Heb 10: 23), reminding us to put all our trust in God. When He says: 'Seek first the kingdom of God and all these things shall be added to you' (Mat 6:33), He expects us to seek the kingdom and desire

Events

CHAPTER 16

nothing else. When He says: 'Ask and you shall receive, seek and you shall find' (Mat 7:7), He wants us to ask with complete trust that we will receive. When God makes a promise, we must have complete faith in His word.

HAGAR ESCAPES

Once Hagar conceives, she starts to arrogantly despise Sarai for her bareness. This angers Sarai, who in turn vents her frustration out on Abram. From Sarai's perspective, she has made a huge sacrifice to ensure that her husband has offspring and is instead repaid with rudeness. Abram should have shown more compassion and respect for his spouse by defending her in the presence of Hagar. Eventually, however, Abram scolds Hagar who flees from the presence of Sarai.

In verses 7-11, the Angel of the Lord appears to Hagar and addresses her with her name and title; 'Hagar, Sarai's maid'. The Angel does this to humble her and remind her of the error of her actions. The fathers believe that Hagar received the just punishment for

> **What the Fathers Say**
>
> When the time comes for us to depart from this world, God will not ask us why we sinned, rather He will ask us, why did you not repent?
>
> – Pope Shenouda III

Ishmael in the Bible

People, Places &Things

The word Ishmael means "God who listened" in Hebrew, indicating that God remained faithful to Abraham and granted him the child that he earnestly desired. However, the fulfillment of God's promise was not made entirely true until the birth of Isaac from Sarai many years later! According to the Christian faith, we believe that we are descendants of "Abraham, Isaac and Jacob". Meanwhile, it is believed that Ishmael was the forefather of all the Arab populations, and from Ishmael's lineage the religion of Islam originated.

Rest assured and do not think too much about any matter. Leave it to God who is in control. Have you ever heard of anyone who has trusted in God, and failed? Impossible

– Pope Kyrillos VI

her actions, and that God approved of this to teach her a lesson. Two important messages come out of this. Firstly, to respect our elders and to display humility towards them. Secondly, we should learn not to take God's blessings for granted, but rather thank Him at all times. Whatever good we have, we should ascribe this to God. All good comes from God, and the more thankful we are, the more God's heart will be moved towards us with compassion, and the more He will be willing to give us.

GOD'S LOVE FOR SINNERS

Even though Hagar sinned, the angel of God still appears to her once she escapes. This displays another of God's intriguing characteristics. Even though Hagar fell into the sin of pride and was forced to suffer the consequences of her actions, God was the one who sought after her during her time of distress. He came to Hagar and listened to her woes, before giving her instructions to return home. In fact, Ishmael means 'God who listened', demonstrating God's compassion towards Hagar, and all sinners in general. This teaches us that even in the midst of our sin, God is still searching for us. In the famous image of Christ knocking on the door, the door knob appears only on the inside of the door. We are the only one who can open for Christ, and regardless of how sinful we are, He is more than willing to enter our hearts once we can accept Him in.

FROM AZMY TO METROPOLITAN BENJAMIN

There is a famous story of a youth called Azmy who lived in Egypt. This man had a notorious reputation amongst his village, was a friend to the sinners and even scoffed at the mere idea of ever entering church. Meanwhile, Azmy's older brother was favoured by both God and men, and lived a life of righteousness and Christian struggle. God willed that Azmy's brother was to fall ill and die at a young age. Whilst in the funeral, Azmy was carrying his brother's casket where he overheard those around him whisper: "How could God take the soul of this saint and leave us with this devilish brother, who is despised by all men?".

Upon hearing these words, Azmy felt that his heart had been pierced, and made a covenant with himself that he would change. He returned home and began reading and studying the story of St. Moses the Strong; his story affected him so deeply that within months he decided to join the monastery of Paramos in Egypt. In 1950, God chose this repentant youth to be ordained a metropolitan, Metropolitan Benjamin, over the diocese of Menufia. Known for his angelic voice, he was given the nickname "Harp of the Church"- he chanted the liturgy so beautifully that hundreds began entering the church and many sinful youth returned to Christ. This shows us how God is always willing to turn us back to Him, even if we ourselves are not diligently seeking Him!

REFLECTION

How often do we lose hope in our spiritual lives, and feel as if God has abandoned us or we are too sinful for God to accept us? Let us instead rest assured and have complete faith and confidence in God's infinite love, remembering that He is always actively seeking us to return to Him!

CHAPTER 17

Events

CHAPTER 17

ABRAM BECOMES ABRAHAM

This chapter starts with yet another meeting between God and Abram. Once again the topic of conversation is that Abram will conceive a son, but by this time Abram is 99 years old. Abram was 75 when God first appeared to him with the promise of a son, and this is now God's third appearance to discuss the matter. This means that Abram had been waiting for almost 25 years for God's promise to come to fruition- a testament to his unwavering faith and belief in the promises of God.

However, before God reveals his forthcoming plan to Abram, a change is required. Strangely enough, God decides to change Abram's name to Abraham. Now why is this the case? The fathers believe that 'Abraham' means the 'Father of the multitude', indicating that the fulfilment of the promise is about to take place. God also instructs Abraham: 'I am Almighty God; walk before Me and be blameless' (verse 1). To walk before the Lord reflected a remarkable display of faith for Abraham, considering that the people of the Old Testament could not comprehend or perceive God the way we do today. It would have been so easy for Abraham to give up on God after 25 years of waiting, but He continued to believe in God and received his reward in due time. Imagine waiting and praying for 25 years, without receiving any tangible reward or sign that your prayer is being answered. This is exactly what happened to Abraham, but he never gave up on the Lord!

THE COVENANT

After His promise to grant Abraham a son, God is not finished.. God makes a covenant with Abraham that every male in his household must be circumcised (verse 10). This involved cutting off the foreskin of the penis, symbolising the person's acceptance into the Jewish community of faith. The fathers tell us that the circumcision of the flesh was symbolic of the circumcision of the heart, mind and soul. God uses a physical sign to show us that He approves of the spiritual works which we have done. However, it is important to note that circumcision in itself was not the covenant, but merely symbolic of it.

Now why did the God instruct Abraham to cut the foreskin of the penis in particular? This bodily member is associated with reproduction and the seed that brings forth children- so God tells them to give birth in

What the Fathers Say

We have to shed what is unnecessary. We have to be willing to bleed. Only then can we belong in his family

– Fr Yacoub Magdy

From Sarai to Sarah

Abram's name is not the only one to be changed in this chapter. God also changes Sarai's name to Sarah. This is the first time God openly involves Sarah in the covenant. Sarai means 'My Princess' but Sarah means 'Princess', *implying that Sarah went from being Abraham's princess only to being the princess (and mother) of everyone. This depicts the completion of God's promise, from which Abraham and Sarah eventually conceived and give birth to Isaac.*

People, Places &Things

The purity of a youth can move the hand of God. It can make the hand of God move mountains

– Fr Yacoub Magdy

the faith. He is stressing the importance of having children born into the faith, into the covenant. God asked Abraham to be circumcised before Isaac comes since Isaac will be the son of the covenant and from his seed, the chosen nation will enter the world. Also, the circumcision was to be performed with a stone knife to remind us that Christ is the chief cornerstone, and the blood which was shed during circumcision reminds us of the blood which Christ would eventually shed for us on the Cross.

CIRCUMCISION AND PURITY

In the Old Testament, circumcision was performed as a symbol of purity and dedication to God. However, in the New Testament, we have the blood of Christ which purifies us and removes every stain of sin from our hearts. Now it is impossible for us to experience God's love and enjoy His divine power whilst we are in a state of impurity. If we find ourselves in unhealthy relationships, watching inappropriate programs and websites and falling into various other sexual sins, then we can rest assured that we will not receive divine power and comfort from God.

Meanwhile, when we flee from these various sins and remove sexual and sensual pleasures from our hearts, only then can we truly experience God's love and comfort. In the beatitudes, Jesus says "Blessed are the pure in heart, for they shall see God" (Mat 5:8) This means that without a pure heart, we cannot see God. It's simple. To take a materialistic example, how can one see the sunrise with bloodshot eyes. Instead, one must first make his eyes healthy, then this light will be a joy to him. Otherwise, if his eyes are unhealthy, this light will be a torment. We must first clean ourselves from within and empty ourselves from lust, and only then will God fill us with His joy and divine comfort.

REFLECTION

How easy is it for us to fall into sexual sins even if it's not adultery or fornication, even making inappropriate jokes or watching bad programs on the TV or the internet? Let's strive to cut off all trace of sexual sin and impurity, in order to empty our hearts for God and God alone.

CHAPTER 18

Events

CHAPTER 18

ABRAHAM MEETS GOD

Chapter 18 marks an extremely important event in the life of Abraham. In verses 1-3, the Lord God appears to Abraham. The word 'Lord' is mentioned in both verses 1 and 3, but with different Hebrew meanings. In verse 1, Moses uses the Hebrew word 'Yahweh' to show that it is an appearance of God to Abraham. However, in verse 3, Abraham uses the Hebrew word 'Adonai', a title of honour which shows that at this point, Abraham is unaware that God Himself had appeared to him with his two angels. If Abraham had known that it was God and his angels, he would not have offered them any food or drink, or even washed their feet. At this stage, Abraham treats them as mere man, unaware of their divine nature.

But out of all people, why was Abraham made worthy to see God? There are three conditions which he met, which we too must meet, to receive such eternal blessing. Firstly, Abraham 'ran from the tent door' (verse 2) to meet his guests. Abraham was at his tent, which resembles the flesh. He flees to greet the visitors. So when Abraham is away from the flesh (desires and lusts of the body), he sees God. We too must be free of any carnal and sensual pleasures in order to see God. Secondly, it was the 'heat of the day', around the 6th hour. This is the same time as the crucifixion, and therefore we can only see God when we take up our cross. This involves making sacrifices; for example, forcing ourselves to keep on praying or to keep on reading our Bible. Finally, despite his old age and the heat, Abraham ran outside with zeal and enthusiasm to meet them. We must exert ourselves in the service of others and have a sacrificial love for them in order to see God. Abraham does not offer them a morsel of bread, but in fact prepares a feast for them (with cakes and the calf)- a real life example of going the extra mile.

SERVING OTHERS

This story is a practical example of what is mentioned in Hebrews 13:2, 'Do not forget to entertain strangers, for by so doing some have unwittingly entertained angels.' In Abraham's eyes, he was simply being hospitable. However, in reality, he was hosting God and his angels. A priest once told a symbolic story of a homeless man who went to attend the midnight Christmas service at church. Whilst everyone was all dressed up in their best clothing, this simple man arrived

> **What the Fathers Say**
>
> *We can do no great things, only small things with great love*
>
> *– Mother Teresa*

Shall I hide from Abraham what I am doing?

Observe the great phenomenon which takes place in this chapter. The Lord God, in His great humility, does not want to make any decision or take any action without first seeking permission and favour from His servant Abraham. God is not obliged to do this at all, He is God, and can do whatever He wishes without permission or approval from anyone. But He does this as a reward to Abraham for his faithfulness and loyalty towards Him. This reminds us of the words in Psalm 25:14 "The secret of the Lord is with those who fear Him, and He will reveal His covenant to them". By being loyal to God through following His commandments and spending time with Him in prayer, Bible reading etc., we too can receive this divine power to know and understand the heart of God.

> **People, Places &Things**

What the Fathers Say

Prayer is capable of doing all things for it manages the hands of Him who controls the universe

— Pope Kyrillos VI

at church with dirty and ragged clothes. After the service, a rich youth invited him over to celebrate Christmas with his family. This displeased the family of the youth, who were insulted and asked the homeless man to leave immediately. Instead, the youth took the homeless man into his bedroom and prepared a small meal for them to share. The youth then began to eat, looked at the homeless man's hands and saw the marks of nails- just like those of Christ on the cross. The homeless man (who was in fact Jesus Christ) immediately disappeared, and the youth rejoiced that he was considered worthy of seeing Christ in the flesh. This story reiterates the Lord Jesus Christ's words in the Bible: "Inasmuch as you did it to one of the least of my brethren, you did it to Me" (Mat 25:40).

ABRAHAM PLEADS FOR SODOM AND GOMORRAH

After this, God reveals his plan to destroy Sodom and Gomorrah for their sexual sin (namely homosexuality). In verses 20-22, the Lord says that the 'outcry against Sodom and Gomorrah is great'. But who is crying out? It wasn't humanity, because man had become so sinful that they were not even speaking to God. The creation is crying out because it was angry at the behaviour of man. Creation cannot tolerate sin because it's against the nature given to it by God. The people of Sodom were not only sinning but committing unnatural acts. Even animals don't behave in such a way! At the crucifixion, the Sun darkened, the rocks split and the earth quaked because nature was disgusted at what man was doing to the Creator. Likewise, Sodom and Gomorrah had become so sinful that even emotionless nature cried out to God in fury and anger.

In verses 23-33, Abraham negotiates with God for the people of Sodom and Gomorrah. Even though God already knows the people well, he allows Abraham to speak out for them. Abraham continues to negotiate and God agrees to Abraham's suggestion each time. This shows us that God is willing to answer our prayers. Now notice the difference between Abraham's request and God's response: Abraham is asking God, 'will you destroy the good with the bad?'. But God's response is 'no I will save the bad for the sake of the good'. This shows the greatness of God's mercy! Logic would say take out the ten good and destroy the rest, but God's mercy opposes this idea- He is willing to save the bad on behalf of those who are good. This demonstrates to those who say God was harsh in the Old Testament how wrong they are.

ST. AUGUSTINE AND ST. MONICA

Finally, this section of the passage teaches us the importance of praying for each other. People often question: Why should we pray for each other or ask the saints to pray for us? Abraham prayed on behalf of the people, and God was willing to lift his wrath

> **What the Fathers Say**
>
> *God has promised forgiveness to your repentance, but He has not promised tomorrow to your procrastination*
>
> *- St. Augustine*

on them. Similarly, the prayers of St. Monica were able to change the heart of God and grant repentance to her son St. Augustine, who was once a sinful, fornicating man on a "pitiful fall into the depths of hell" (according to his own autobiography). His mother, seeing this, prayed and cried with tears daily for the repentance of her son. In the Confessions of St. Augustine, he later wrote: "But you sent down from above help and rescued my soul from the depths of this darkness because my mother, your faithful servant, wept to you for me, shedding more tears for my spiritual death than other mothers shed for the bodily death of a son". After his repentance, Augustine was ordained a bishop, with his own son (who was born out of wed lock) sitting right beside him!

REFLECTION

How many times do I stand before God in prayer and really have 100% faith that I am standing before the King of Kings, who is capable of answering all my prayers?

CHAPTER 19

GOD APPEARS TO LOT

In chapter 19, Lot is visited by the same two angels that visited Abraham in the previous chapter. Just like Abraham, Lot is unaware of their divine nature but still rises to greet them and humbles himself by bowing down to them- a sign of respect. Lot insists that the strangers come to his house so that they can take rest and he prepares for them a feast. Here, Lot is showing the same hospitality displayed by his uncle Abraham in the previous chapter. Even though he resides amongst sinners, he hasn't forgotten all the good that he learned from Abraham. Also, Lot knows how bad the city is and wants to protect the strangers from any temptations and trials which may await them.

In verses 4-11, the men of Sodom and Gomorrah arrive at Lot's house, waiting for him to release the strangers so that they can engage in homosexual acts with them. Lot in turn does something extremely strange by offering his daughters to the men instead. Why does Lot do this? Because in Lot's time, it was the responsibility of the homeowner to protect the guest at all costs. Hence, Lot negotiates with the men and offers his daughters to protect the visitors. However, unlike Abraham who negotiated with God, Lot negotiated with evil. Lot was never going to win if the angels hadn't dragged him inside. We can never win in a negotiation with the devil. When faced with sin, our safest option

Events

CHAPTER 19

is to flee to God in prayer, who alone can protect us from every temptation.

But why did God Himself appear to Abraham and not Lot? Because it wouldn't be possible for God to enter such a sinful city- therefore He sent two angels instead. Being in the presence of God requires a pure heart. Lot was not a bad person. He was hospitable and knew how to distinguish between what is sinful and what is not. His main weakness was that he enjoyed the easy life- the very reason he chose Sodom in the first place. The fathers believe that Sodom would have destroyed Lot if God did not destroy Sodom. Lot loved the easy life and exposed himself to homosexual acts and the need to bargain with the abuse of his daughters as a result. Even while in danger, Lot argues that he would rather flee to a small nearby city than the mountains (verse 20). When we compromise with sin, we expose ourselves to unnecessary problems

Lot's wife: a pillar of salt?

Interestingly, the name of Lot's wife is not given in the Bible, even though her life provides many lessons. We are not told of the real reason she looked back to the city as it was being destroyed- some believe she was looking to see if her daughters were following behind, while others say she was simply too attached to her previous life and did not want to leave it behind once and for all. Either way, the story of Lot's wife becoming a pillar of salt teaches us the consequences of looking back on our previous sins. Once we have committed a sin, repented in front of God and confessed in front of our confession father, we must move and completely forget about the sin. In the reconciliation prayer, we ask God to remove from us "every memory of evil entailing death"; meaning that even the memory of sin should be erased from our minds.

People, Places & Things

GENESIS FOR TEENS

and it becomes impossible for us to taste God's divine love and comfort.

GOD SAVES LOT

Even though St. Peter called Lot "righteous" (2 Peter 2:7), as mentioned above, Lot's weakness was the easy life. This is shown in verses 12-15, where his married daughters and sons-in-law refuse to take him seriously when told to flee. Even Lot himself was slow to escape, and had to be hurried and forced by the angels, who grabbed his hand and led him out of Sodom (verses 16-18). This shows the love of God who will still save us, even if we are half-hearted with our efforts.

In the stories of the desert fathers, there was a rich and evil man by the name of Peter. This man had no good works, and lived his life in continual enjoyment and pleasure. Once a poor beggar came and knocked on his door, pleading with him for food. He initially refused, but due to the man's persistence, Peter grabbed a loaf of bread and smacked him across the head with it. That same day in his sleep, Peter had a vision of the divine judgement. One angel came and placed all his evil works on one end of a scale. Another angel was then entrusted with placing all of Peter's good works on the other end of the scale. Struggling to find anything, the angel eventually found the loaf of bread with which Peter smacked the beggar and exclaimed 'this is the only good I could find'. Immediately, Peter awoke from his sleep in fear, sold all his

What the Fathers Say

Three men came to Abraham in the heat of the day, but to Lot, two angels came in the evening, as it was not possible for Lot to get the whole splendour of daylight that Abraham could get. To Abraham, the Lord came with the two angels. While to Lot, only the two angels came. Lot received the two destroyers, while Abraham received the Saviour together with the destroyers"

- Origen

possessions and became a monk. This teaches that God is willing to use even our smallest efforts (even a piece of bread) to grant us salvation and to glorify His name.

LOT'S LINEAGE PRESERVED

In verses 30-38, Lot's daughters get him drunk and lie with him. This reminds us of the story of Noah who also got drunk and exposed his nakedness (Genesis 9). To a certain extent, the mistakes of the past are being repeated. Even though some excuse the daughters as naïve girls who wanted to preserve the lineage of their father, they went about their intention in the completely wrong way. A wrong should not be corrected with another wrong. There is no room for this sort of thinking in a faithful person. If the girls had faith they would have realised that God had other ways of preserving Lot's lineage. Sometimes we use our own logic when making a decision, forgetting that God is in total control of the situation. In these situations, it is best to pray, consult our elders, (confession father) and leave the matter completely in God's hands.

> **What the Fathers Say**
>
> Let us not look back and heed Satan's invitation to withdraw; but look ahead to where the Lord Christ invites us. Let us lift our eyes towards heaven. So as not be deceived by the earth and its vain pleasures
>
> – St Cyprian

REFLECTION

How often do I fall into despair, looking back and remembering all my previous sins? This is one of Satan's biggest traps, which he uses to prevent us from repenting and returning back to God. Let us remember that Christ's blood on the Cross has removed all our sins, and have joy in this!

CHAPTER 20

Events

CHAPTER 20

ABRAHAM LIES AGAIN

This chapter is pretty much a repeat of the story in chapter 12, where Abraham claimed that Sarah was his sister (rather than wife) out of fear of death. Abraham is yet to overcome this fear of death, and displays this in yet another lie! Even though Abraham was an amazing man, as a human he still had some weaknesses. The only One who is perfect is Christ. No matter how good any of us become, we all have little weaknesses. David committed adultery, Thomas doubted and Peter denied but they all eventually became heroes of our faith. This teaches us that we should never despair, but rather endure our weaknesses patiently and pray that God helps us to overcome them.

There is a story of a monk who was always attacked with lustful and bodily pleasures. He would often fall into sinful thoughts, and would struggle to overcome these temptations. Even though he exerted himself in much asceticism and prayer to fight these satanic battles, such thoughts never left him until the day of his death. This caused him much despair, however, he never lost hope and continued to struggle against the devil. On the day of his death, he heard a voice from heaven exclaiming 'You are blessed O father, for you fought sin all your life and have become worthy of the kingdom of heaven'. This teaches us that even though we will be faced with weakness all the days of our lives, God is faithful in helping us to overcome. And even if we feel that we are not victorious at the time of sin, God observes our repeated struggle and repentance and prepares crowns for us in heaven because of this.

GOD PROTECTS HIS COVENANT

Abraham's second lie happens just before Isaac's birth from Sarah. God wants no doubt about the parentage of Isaac by ensuring that everyone is clear that no one touched Sarah intentionally (Pharaoh in chapter 12) or unintentionally (Abimelech in this chapter). In both cases, God stopped them from coming near her. This shows that God is not only capable of allowing the barren to give birth, but protecting His covenant and promise, despite our sins! God stopped Pharaoh by sending a plague and God stops Abimelech by giving him an illness.

> **What the Fathers Say**
>
> "All of us sin constantly. We slip and fall. It is important to get up immediately after a fall and to keep on walking towards God. Even if we fall a hundred times a day, it does not matter. We must get up, and go on walking towards…

Isaac… a symbol of Christ?

Notice that even though Abraham lies about his wife (not once but twice), God still protects His covenant to ensure that no one doubts the parentage of Isaac. God wants to make sure that everyone is clear that no one touched Sarah. Now consider this; Isaac was born of an elderly woman, and God had to open up her womb. He was the son of promise, made possible by the will and act of God. Even though Abraham was 99 and Sarah was 90, God made it possible for them to have Isaac. Now consider Christ, born of a virgin with no male involvement. The Holy Spirit purified St. Mary's womb and He too, was born in a miraculous fashion. Isaac is a typology of Christ, Sarah a typology of St. Mary and Abraham a typology of God. Abraham represents the Father, and no other man is allowed to touch the woman from whom would come the son of promise. Under no circumstance was Sarah touched by anyone, just like St. Mary herself was a virgin all her life!

> **People, Places & Things**

What the Fathers Say

...God without looking back. What has happened has happened, it is in the past

– Elder Thaddeus of Vitovnica

In verse 6, God says to Abimelech: 'For I also withheld you from sinning against Me'. Now why does God say, 'sinning against Me' rather than 'sinning against Abraham' or 'sinning against Sarah'? This is because we are God's people, and when anything happens to us, it happens to Him. Likewise, whatever deeds we do to others, we do to God. Recall when Christ appeared to Saul in Acts 9- He asked him: 'Saul, Saul. Why are you persecuting ME?' (verse 4). God calls us part of Him and He is part of us. This is a source of great comfort, that we are in communion with God. That God loves us so much, that if someone attacks us or tries to harm us, they are attacking and harming God Himself. Now how can we maintain this constant fellowship and communion with God. By keeping the sacraments, remaining diligent in prayer and Bible reading and leading a life of repentance.

REFLECTION

Why do I often take matters into my own hands, instead of trusting in God's divine promises and love. "He who promises is faithful" (Heb 10:23) Do I really believe and live this faith out each and every day?

CHAPTER 21

ISAAC IS BORN

Previously, when God appeared to Abraham in chapter 18, He promised Abraham that he would bear a son. That appearance was a physical appearance of God in front of Abraham. Likewise in this chapter, God visits Sarah, but this time, it is not a physical appearance, rather it was to bless and open her womb. God's visit was proven by Sarah's womb becoming fertile. Some visits from God were full appearances, while others were indicated by an action. God's visit to Sarah was to show that if He can reawaken a barren womb, then He can definitely allow a virgin to conceive a child. Hence, the birth of Isaac is a typology and symbolism for the coming birth of Christ.

Sarah conceives a son and calls him 'Isaac', meaning laughter. In Hebrew, this implies that laughter comes from joy. Sarah was joyous at the miraculous birth of Isaac and the fulfilment of God's faithful promise. In verse 4, Abraham circumcised Isaac at 8 days of age. This is significant. Just like God kept His promise of a child, Abraham keeps his end of the promise and circumcises the child, the seal and confirmation of faith at the time. This demonstrates the true nature of a relationship with God. We should not come to God only when we need Him, but also to thank Him, praise Him and honour Him as well.

Events

CHAPTER 21

SARAH VS HAGAR

In verses 10-14, Sarah asks Abraham to cast out Hagar and Ishmael. Her request is very direct and Abraham is not pleased by such demands. He is reacting as a father who loves and cares for his son. However, God tells Abraham to heed Sarah's request and he obeys immediately. Abraham compromises his feelings of loss for his son by submitting the matter entirely into God's hands in complete obedience and faith. Abraham was being prepared by God for the sacrifice of Isaac, which was yet to come. God trains us to give through small steps before taking a huge leap. We all have some faith, and accepting God's requests is a test of this faith. Even though it is painful at times, we must

Hagar: she who speaks with God

After the birth of Isaac, Sarah is concerned that her son will not receive the whole inheritance from Abraham, and that this instead will have to be shared with Ishmael. Sarah perceives this threat, and without any justified reasoning, asks Abraham to expel Hagar and her son Ishmael. Abraham reluctantly adheres to the words of his wife, being encouraged to do so by God and expels both Hagar and Ishmael. He provides provisions for Hagar and her son, but these are limited and eventually Hagar places her son underneath a bush, so that at least he will die in the shade.

Hagar weeps, and her son lifts up his voice and cries out. His name is Ishmael, meaning 'God hears', and God certainly heard his cries this time. The angel of the Lord calls her by name: "What ails you Hagar?", reassures her: "Fear not", reminds her of his promise: "I will make him a great nation" and even opened her eyes to see a well that she didn't notice before. See the mercy of God! Even though Hagar was rejected and despised by man, she was never ever forgotten by God!

People, Places &Things

What the Fathers Say

Never lose hope; however lifeless you may be, for 'God is able to raise up children to Abraham from these stones' (Mat 3: 9), and without a doubt you are better than many stones"

— Pope Shenouda III

prove our faith by detaching ourselves from anything worldly and submitting ourselves completely to God's will.

But this poses some interesting questions. Why did Ishmael have to leave Abraham's household? Why couldn't he be heir with Isaac? This is because Hagar and Ishmael lived in Arabia (Mount Sinai), which is where Moses received the law. Therefore, Ishmael represents those who are under the Law. The Law cannot save- instead, its puts you under the bondage of sin. However, Isaac represents the grace and new covenant, i.e. Christ. As children of Christ, we have become freed from the bondage of sin.

THE POWER OF PRAYER

It is also interesting to note that Hagar (representing the law) could not save her own son in verses 15-17. All she could do was go to the wilderness and cry out. God listened to the cries of Ishmael but not Hagar. This shows us that the law itself cannot save the people under it but if the people cry, God will listen to them and give them a spring (the Holy Spirit) who will guide them. Ishmael cried out and God saved Him and made him a great nation. Likewise, all of us can be saved if we cry out to God.

In Psalm 13, David the psalmist cries out in agony: 'How long O Lord do You forget me forever. How long do You hide Your face from me?' (verse 1). Meanwhile, at the end of the psalm, he cries out in joy: 'I will sing to the Lord, Because He has dealt bountifully with me' (verse 6). Now what is the reason behind this rapid transformation? It is David's complete faith that His prayer is heard and acceptable in the eyes of God. If we display similar faith when we cry out to Him, then no doubt our prayers will be accepted if they in accordance with His will.

REFLECTION

How often in life ?? do I find myself like Hagar- alone, desperate and seemingly hopeless? What is my response to these situations? We should learn from Hagar, and cry out to God in genuine tears, asking and having compete faith in his love and mercy.

What the Fathers Say

Indeed, God has many solutions. We think of our problems with our human mind, and our mind is limited. As for God, His knowledge and wisdom have no limits. When matters become difficult, the difficulty is relative, that is for us as human beings. As for God, there is nothing difficult. Everything is easy, and the solutions are numerous

— Pope Shenouda III

CHAPTER 22

Events

CHAPTER 22

SACRIFICING ISAAC

In the first two verses of this chapter, God is having an actual conversation with Abraham because he is about to embark on the toughest test of his life and there can be no room for any doubt or confusion concerning God's request. God asks Abraham to 1. Take his son, 2. His only son, 3. Isaac (stressing exactly who), 4. Whom he loves. God's test for Abraham is extremely hard and God understands this, hence the clear instructions given. This was the request from God. If Abraham passed this test, he would enjoy an everlasting relationship with God. This was not only a test of Abraham's faith, but a test of his love for God.

Notice how seriously Abraham takes this test. In verse 3, he rises early in the morning, showing us that he took God's request seriously. He then cuts the wood, not entrusting any of his servants with the task but instead doing it himself. Abraham is drinking the whole bitter cup. Just like God planned man's salvation and prepared the Cross, Abraham is planning everything for the eventual sacrifice of his son. Furthermore, in verse 4, Abraham walks for 3 days, suffering the whole way because he knows that he is about to kill his son. He was in deep agony presenting his son, as if he himself was also being sacrificed. The same way, the Father shared in the agony of the Son on the Cross while being sacrificed. And just as Abraham walked three days with Isaac his son, so too does Christ spent three days in the tomb before His resurrection. Similarly, the wood placed on Isaac's shoulders resembles the wood of the Cross which was in fact carried by Christ.

In verse 5, Abraham instructs his servants: 'I will go yonder and worship and we will come back to you'. If Abraham knew that he was going to kill Isaac, what does he mean by 'WE' will come back to you? Abraham considered that somehow God was able to raise Isaac, even from the dead. Notice this tremendous display of faith! Abraham's faith set no limits for what God could do, even though at the time, raising someone from the dead was completely unheard of. Since Isaac came from a dead womb, Abraham had no problem believing that God would raise him from the dead. Abraham truly believed that Isaac would return with him! It is important to also admire the obedience of Isaac (believed

The Ultimate Sacrifice: Holy Thursday of Passion Week

God instructs Abraham to make the ultimate sacrifice, and in complete submission and obedience, Abraham prepares to offer his son Isaac to God. Abraham feared God to the extent of offering his only son, and God reciprocated this love one-hundred fold. Not only did God grant him descendants as the sand of the sea, but by offering his son Isaac, God revealed to Abraham a glimpse of salvation and the ultimate sacrifice which had been prepared since the foundation of the world, (the Cross). Truly, the words of David the psalmist are true: "The secret of the Lord is with them that fear him; and He reveals His covenant to them" (Psalm 25: 14). This event is so important that our Orthodox Church commemorates the sacrifice of Abraham on Holy Thursday of passion week every single year!

People, Places &Things

Thus, the slaying of Isaac was a type of the shedding of the Blood of Christ, the Son of God, on the cross, for the salvation of the world. And as Isaac carried the firewood for the burnt offering, likewise, Christ carried the wood of the Cross. And as Isaac returned alive, likewise Christ rose living, from the dead, and appeared to His holy disciples

— Fraction for Covenant Thursday

to be in his late twenties to early thirties at the time). On no occasion does he even consider questioning his father's actions, but rather he accepts everything in submissiveness and obedience.

ABRAHAM'S LOVE REVEALED

After God appears to Abraham and prevents him from following through with the sacrifice, God exclaims: 'for now I know that you fear God, since you have not withheld your son, your only son, from Me' (verse 12). This doesn't mean that God didn't know about Abraham's love beforehand, for God knows everything and cannot gain new knowledge. Instead, God is revealing what He already knows about us though we don't even know it ourselves. Just like a parent knows that their child is capable but doesn't say anything until the child discovers it for themselves, so too does God reveal to Abraham the extent of his zealous faith and love.

ABRAHAM'S SACRIFICE AND THE CROSS

The Fathers believe that verse 13 is an account of what happened at the Cross. The two horns of the ram caught in the thicket remind us of Christ's two arms, lifted and attached to the Cross. Picture the scene; in front of Abraham is Isaac lying on the altar, but still alive. Behind Abraham is the ram caught in thicket and about to be sacrificed. Abraham is between them. This brings us to an intriguing analogy. Christ is both fully divine and human. On the Cross, His divinity never separated from His humanity. Hence, the fathers see Isaac as representing the Son of God who obeyed His Father up to the point of death, but doesn't die, because the divine nature of Christ does not die. The ram represents the Son of God in the flesh, the human nature of Christ which died on the cross. Isaac and the ram represent the Son in the divine nature (which doesn't die) and the human nature (which died on the Cross) respectively. The two are together to symbolise that the divine and human nature of Christ never separated, not even for a single instant.

What the Fathers Say

At this moment, the words of the son, 'My father!' embodies the severest situation of that experience. Imagine to what extent does the voice of the son to be slain tear out the heart of his father! Yet Abraham's steadfast faith did not keep him from saying tenderly: 'Here I am my son!'

– Origen

REFLECTION

Abraham was obedient to the extent of offering his only son Isaac to the slaughter, yet I find it so difficult to give up time, pleasure, luxury and even sin for God! Next time I find myself attached to a certain sin or possession, remember that Abraham was even willing to over his only son for God.

CHAPTER 23

Events

Sarah is dead

After God spared Isaac's life in the previous chapter, Abraham is faced with another calamity: the death of his wife Sarah. She was 127 years old at her death, and died in Hebron in the land of Canaan. However, since Abraham's focus was on the heavenly home (rather than the earthly), he did not own any land in Hebron and wandered around as God guided him. Thus, when Sarah died, he approached the people of Hebron and asked if he could purchase land in order to properly bury his wife. Abraham was so respected among the people that they tried to give him the land for free, but he refused and payed its full worth. This burial plot would eventually bury not only Sarah, but Isaac, Rebekah, Leah, Jacob and even Abraham himself.

Lessons to be learned

Even though this is an extremely simple story, there are many lessons to be learnt from it. Abraham mourned Sarah and wept for her, displaying his love and sincerity towards her. It is important for us to show love for one another and to share in other people's emotions; to be happy with the joyful and weep with those who mourn.

It is also important to note that until now, Abraham had not bought any land or set down any roots on earth because his complete focus is on heaven only. In the book of Hebrews 11: 9-10, St. Paul describes Abraham as having 'dwelt in the land of promise as in a foreign country, dwelling in tents with Isaac and Jacob... for he waited for the city which has foundations, whose builder and maker is God'. This is a lesson in practical asceticism. You don't have to be a monk or nun to detach yourself from the world and its pleasures.

Abraham was married and had children, yet he considered all earthly possessions as useless so that he might gain God's favour. He was so obedient to God, that when God asked him to leave his home town, he left with no hesitation (chapter 12). Abraham did not even have a place of his own to bury his beloved wife Sarah! Perhaps this is what made Abraham so beloved to God! He obeyed without complaint and had complete and perfect faith in God, never questioning anything! Therefore, God venerated the name of Abraham so much and blessed him beyond all measure.

What the Fathers Say

What is dying? Just what it is to put off a garment. For the body is about the soul as a garment; and after laying this aside for a short time by means of death, we shall resume it again with more splendour

– St John Chrysostom

The Promised Land: Canaan

Chapter 23 begins by telling us that Sarah died in Kirjath Arba (Hebron), in the land of Canaan. It ends with verse 19 informing us that Abraham buried Sarah his wife in the cave of the field of Macphelah (Hebron), also in the land of Canaan. Now this is extremely important! Abraham insisted for Sarah to be buried in the land of Canaan. This was also known as the "Promised Land", the land which God promised to give to Abraham and his descendants in Genesis 12: 1-3 and again in Genesis 15: 18-21. This shows us that Abraham believed in life after death and he knew that Sarah would rise again, and wanted to her to rise in the land which God promised to Abraham and his descendants. This teaches us the power of resurrection and belief in life after death.

People, Places &Things

What the Fathers Say

I want nothing from the world for the world has nothing to be desired, only temptations for the beginners. I want nothing of the world, for the world is too poor to give me. If what I want is available in the world, the world would be a heaven. But it is still an earth as I see, there is nothing in it except material things. In fact, I search for the heavenly matters, for the Spirit of God.

– Pope Shenouda III

ST. PAUL THE HERMIT

A perfect example of someone who detached himself from the world is St. Paul the first hermit. After the death of his parents, he and his brother disagreed over the distribution of their parent's wealth. They took the matter to court, and as St. Paul was walking towards the courtroom, he saw a family mourning over the death of one of their members. St. Paul then considered the vanity and futility of this world, and the result of man's life here on earth, death. Immediately, St. Paul decided to give his brother the entire share of his parent's wealth, and fled to live a life of solitude in the desert alone. He desired nothing from the world, and sought after one ultimate goal: a life with Christ.

REFLECTION

At times, I become so caught up with the world and its desires that I completely forget about God. But do I ever remember the words of St. Paul, who reminds us to "Not love the world, nor the things in the world. For if anyone loves the world, the love of the Father is not in Him" (1 John 2: 15)

CHAPTER 24

FINDING ISAAC A WIFE

Chapter 24 is one of the longest chapters in Genesis but covers one event in great detail, including finding Isaac a wife. Since Abraham is ageing and Sarah has passed away, it's time for Isaac to marry. It appears that Isaac had been very close to his mother and was feeling her absence. His father was eager to find a companion to fill this void and in turn, continue his bloodline. However, Abraham insists that the bride must be from his homeland in Mesopotamia and sends out his servant to find the appropriate candidate. As this is a rather straightforward story, the fathers find spiritual meaning linked back to Christ and the Church. In this story, Isaac symbolises Christ and Rebekah symbolises the church, an analogy for the betrothal of the Church to Christ.

In verses 1-9, Abraham takes an oath with his servant that Isaac is not to marry from the Canaanites. At the time, when oaths were made, people would swear on the greatest thing or person they knew. The fathers explain that for Abraham, circumcision had become the most holy and sacred covenant between him and God. Hence, in making the covenant, he asks his servant to place his hand under his thigh and thereby swear on the most sacred of covenants. Now why does Abraham insist that Isaac should not take a wife from his homeland? Because when Abraham left his home, he did so at the instruction of God and accepted whole-heartedly, never looking back. We too, after falling into sin or being faced with temptation, should never look back in despair, but rather look towards Christ and build towards a more positive future.

THE POWER OF PRAYER

Upon embarking on his journey, the servant makes an amazing prayer in verses 12-14. This shows us how much faith he has in the God of Abraham. It teaches us as servants of God how we should pray- before the start of every service, during every step of the service and at the end of every service. The servant resembles the disciples in the New Testament, who were likewise successful in their mission because they did everything in the name of Christ. This presents an important practical lesson for us all. We should ensure that prayer becomes the first thing we do every day. Whilst it's so easy to flick through our mobile phones or scroll through Facebook once we wake up, how many of us ensure that the first few minutes of our day are spent in prayer?

Isaac and Rebekah: a Symbol of Christ and the Church

In the same way which Isaac and Rebekah came together, this resembles the coming together of Christ and the church. Just like Father Abraham desired a bride for his son Isaac, so too did God the Father desire for His Son Christ to be wedded to the church. Just like the son Isaac was considered almost dead (Genesis 22) upon Abraham's sacrifice, so too were we (the church) spiritually dead before Christ's sacrifice on the Cross. Just like Isaac was promised before His coming and miraculously conceived, so too was Christ miraculously conceived from a virgin. Finally, just like Rebekah was chosen before she even knew it, so too were we (the church) chosen by Christ to be His children even before our conception.

People, Places &Things

What the Fathers Say

Rebecca used to go every day to the well to draw water; and there she encountered Abraham's servant and got to marry Isaac. Learn to come every day to the well of the Scripture to continuously draw from the water of the Holy Spirit

— Origen

By doing so, this ensures that Christ will bless the day and stand by our side throughout its entirety.

A disciple of St. Joseph the monk once said: 'we observed that the elder would not embark on anything without first praying. We would ask him about something in the future or the next day, and his reply was that he would tell us tomorrow. He would do this so that he could pray first'. This is a practical lesson demonstrating the importance of prayer, which should ultimately guide every step of our lives.

Another modern-day example of prayer comes from Pope Kyrillos the 6th. His prayer life was like none other in the history of our Orthodox Church- he would wake up at around 2 or 3am, pray the midnight praises and matins, then pray the Holy Liturgy every single day, even as Patriarch. He was also a miracle performer, and was given the gift of prophesy. His name is venerated in Egypt and around the world till this day, to the extent that almost everyone alive in Egypt during his patriarchy experienced a miracle or knew someone that experienced a miracle at his holy hands. Whenever his disciples asked him how he performed a certain miracle or how he was able to foresee the future, he would always reply with the verse: "Delight yourself also in the Lord, And He shall give you the desires of your heart" (Psalm 37:4).

REBEKAH'S HOSPITALITY

In verses 16-25, the servant waits for Rebekah to offer water to the camels as well to show that she has the same spirit of service and hospitality as his masters Abraham and Isaac. Rebekah had to work hard to fill the troughs for ten camels, running back and forth to the well numerous times. She chose to fill the pitchers all by herself, not only serving a stranger, but serving his animals as well. Just like Isaac, Rebekah displays humility, hospitality and generosity. She was happy to walk the second mile with others, just like Christ did as well. Because Rebekah displayed the same characteristics as Isaac, she deserved to be his bride. In a similar manner, we can only be joined to Christ when we become like Him and deny ourselves for the sake of our fellow brethren.

It is important to note that in verse 33, the servant refuses to eat or rest until he announces his task. He is on a mission and is focussed- he does not let weariness or earthly desires distract him from his ultimate goal. We too should serve with the same determination and perseverance, being completely focused on God alone. It's so easy to be distracted by politics and gossip within the church community, but the true servant of God ignores all this and desires God alone.

> ## What the Fathers Say
>
> There is no need at all to make long discourses; it is enough to stretch out one's hand and say: 'Lord, as you will, and as you know, have mercy'. And if the conflict grows fiercer say: 'Lord Help!'. God knows very well what we need and He shows us mercy
>
> - Abba Macarius

REFLECTION

What is the role of prayer in my life? Do I recognise its importance, and begin every task with prayer, asking for God's assistance just like the servant of Abraham did?

CHAPTER 25

ABRAHAM TAKES ANOTHER WIFE AND THEN DIES

The start of this chapter sees Abraham taking another wife by the name of Keturah. The scholars explain that in Hebrew, the same word is used for 'wife' and 'woman' and the intended meaning here is 'woman' (as in concubine, rather than wife). Also, the early fathers say that like Hagar before her, Keturah was not a wife of the same level of Sarah. This is confirmed by the following:

1. Abraham only gives gifts to his children from Hagar and Keturah, but the true inheritance was given to Isaac alone.

2. Abraham refused a wife for Isaac from the Canaanite women so he was not about to marry one himself.

3. Abraham's love for Sarah was very deep and he had no desire to replace her after so many years together.

Abraham eventually dies at the age of 175 years old, meaning he lived long enough to see his grandchildren, Esau and Jacob. Now Abraham was buried alone, so how was he 'gathered to his people'? (verse 8). The fathers describe death as merely a move to a different place, so Abraham is being gathered with all his forefathers who had died before him- Noah, Seth and Adam. In our Orthodox liturgy, the priest prays: 'we too who are foreigners in this world, grant us Your peace unto the end'. Our lives here on earth are

Events

CHAPTER 25

only temporary, and our real residence is in heaven, where we too will be gathered with all the saints and angels in praise.

ESAU AND JACOB ARE BORN

In verse 21, Isaac intercedes for his wife Rebekah to open her barren womb. Isaac prayed and he represents Christ who always intercedes for the Church to give her life. God answers these prayers and Rebekah becomes pregnant with twins. However, the twins struggle inside her womb and this has important spiritual symbolism. Since Rebekah represents the church and the twins struggled in her womb, this means that there will always be schisms inside the church. The church will always have divisions and conflicts, but this should not distract us or put us off attending

What the Fathers Say

Abraham departed, and his life was all days, with no nights

- St. Jerome

Jacob I have loved, but Esau I have hated?

This chapter recounts the birth of Jacob and Esau- both extremely notable characters in the Bible. Their lives were not only discussed throughout Genesis, but also in Malachi 1:3, which states: "Jacob I have loved, but Esau I have hated". Now this raises some serious questions. How can God hate? Does God show partiality? Here, the word "love" refers to God's act of choosing Jacob, while "hate" refers to God not choosing Esau. God knows the hearts of all men, and despite the fact that both Jacob and Esau were sinners, Jacob was more obedient to God and more willing to work with God than Esau, who completely rejected God's commandment. Jacob was more receptive to the commandments of God than Esau, and therefore was blessed and "loved" by God. God did not hate Esau the man, for God cannot hate His own children, His creation. God hated the sin which existed within Esau. More about that in the next few chapters though!

People, Places &Things

the services. We should come to church with the sole goal of spiritual growth.

In verse 27, Esau is described as a 'skilful hunter' while Jacob is described as a 'mild man, living in the tents'. Compare this with the first pair of brothers, Cain (a farmer who was blessed) and Abel (a shepherd who wasn't blessed). With Esau and Jacob, the occupations are switched. Esau worked like Abel, but unlike Abel, he was not blessed. Meanwhile, Cain worked on the land like Jacob, but unlike Jacob, was not blessed. Therefore it is not a person's occupation which forms their character, but rather their attitude towards their work and the diligence with which they carry it out.

After this, the boys grow up and Jacob eventually steals Esau's birthright. This raises an extremely interesting question. Did Jacob sin in taking Esau's birthright? The truth is, Esau despised his birthright (verse 34) and did not care for it in the first place. He didn't sell it for a banquet- he sold it for a plain bowl of lentils, meaning that the matter wasn't simply a matter of food. Esau just didn't care about his birthright. He sold it because he didn't care. In a similar way, how often do we give up our Christian faith and beliefs over the smallest and silliest worldly desires and interests.

We must be strong and firm in our resistance against sinful desires. In Psalm 1, David the psalmist says: 'Blessed are those who walk not in the counsel of the ungodly, nor stand in the path of sinners, nor sit in the seat of the scornful'. Notice the progression of the verbs- from 'walks' to 'stands' to 'sits'. If we walk amongst sinners, we will then stand with them and eventually sit and find comfort in their presence. Therefore, it's best to cut the sin off from its root before the sin grows, controls us and then eventually destroys us.

THE 21 LIBYAN MARTYRS

Next time I am faced with the option of denying God and pursuing after sinful and lustful pleasures (whether this be inappropriate websites, videos, gossip, judgement, sinful company etc.), let me remember the example of the 21 Libyan martyrs of 2015. These were ordinary Coptic men, just like us, who were taken captive by Islamic extremists and faced with a choice: to deny their faith in the Lord Christ, or to be slaughtered for their beliefs. Not only this, but they were forced to suffer for forty days beforehand, being placed in an enclosed room with water up to their waist such that whenever they were about to fall asleep, they could not for fear of being submerged in the water and drowning. Such was their faith and loyalty to Christ, that they refused to deny Him. Yet I deny Him over a lustful desire or sinful company?

> ## What the Fathers Say
>
> These 21 martyrs of Libya were martyred. This was not an act of ending life, it was a act of choosing life
>
> – Archbishop Angaelos

REFLECTION

Just like Esau so easily gave away his birthright, how easy is it for me to give up my Christian faith and deny the Lord when faced with even the smallest of temptations. Let us learn from the example of the Libyan martyrs, who were faced with even death, yet shined in their loyalty towards God.

CHAPTER 26

CHAPTER 26

Events

LIKE FATHER, LIKE SON

Chapter 26 shows Isaac following in his father Abraham's footsteps in dealing with certain situations. Isaac not only inherited wealth from Abraham, but also his goodness and his weaknesses. Just like in the days of Abraham, there is now a famine and Isaac's first reaction is the same as that of his father, to run to Egypt and escape. History is repeating itself! The Lord then appeared to Isaac to tell him not to go to Egypt but rather to stay in Canaan, where God would look after him. Again, God is making the same promise to Isaac that He did to Abraham in the generation before him.

What happens in verses 6-9 is even more intriguing! When asked about Rebekah, Isaac calls her his sister rather than his wife out of fear. This is the exact same mistake Abraham made, not once but twice! This shows us that Abraham told Isaac everything that had gone on before his birth (otherwise how would Isaac have known to call Rebekah his sister?). It also shows us that Isaac inherited Abraham's weakness. In the exact same way, as children of Adam and Eve, we inherited both their goodness (being made in the image of God) and their weakness (original sin) which Christ wiped away.

ISAAC VS THE PHILISTINES

In verses 12-16, Isaac does something which his father Abraham never did: he begins to sow the land. This highlights the beginning of the fulfilment of the promise, Isaac is finally starting to inherit the land. However, the Philistines are filled with envy and begin to close Isaac's wells to cut off his flock from their nourishment. Instead of letting this setback stop him, Isaac moves on and digs new wells but again experiences trouble from the people. Isaac then digs another three wells and finally, at the last one, there is no trouble. Isaac didn't quarrel or argue with his persecutors. Instead, he moved away from trouble because his aim was to remain at peace with everyone.

Since Isaac remained peaceful and avoided conflict at all costs, God rewarded him by bringing his enemies under his feet. Towards the end of the chapter, the enemies confess that God is with Isaac and they ask Isaac to promise not to do them any harm. When God is on someone's side, they become invincible. Isaac's response to this situation reminds us of one of the famous beatitudes:

What the Fathers Say

After that, Isaac dug a third well he called 'Rehoboth', saying 'The Lord has made room for us, and we shall be fruitful in the land'. Indeed, Isaac's name has become great in the whole world, because he has filled us with knowledge of the Holy Trinity

– Origen

Scared of Isaac: the fear of the children of God

Notice that Abimelech the King expels Isaac from the land. Why? Abimelech explains this to Isaac: "For you are much mightier than we" (verse 16). This was his immediate response. However, Abimelech instantly regrets this, travelling all the way to make a covenant with Isaac, for "We have certainly seen that the Lord is with you". Isaac overcomes their initial fear with love, making a feast for them. How marvellous is this, for the believer to have a testimonial from those outside, to realise that he is a man of the Lord and to feel that the Lord's dignity surrounds him!

People, Places &Things

‘Blessed are the peacemakers for they shall be called sons of God’ (Mat 5:9).

POPE KYRILLOS: A PEACEMAKER

There is a famous story of an Egyptian newspaper which used to publish false stories about Pope Kyrillos the 6th, ruining his reputation in the eyes of the public. Due to several complaints, the newspaper was forced to shut down. Upon hearing this, Pope Kyrillos' assistant rushed to him exclaiming: ‘Good news Sayedna! The newspaper has finally shut down’. Upon hearing this, Pope Kyrillos became extremely agitated and replied: ‘How is this good news? What about the 200 workers who lost their jobs because of this’. Pope Kyrillos did not care that the newspaper was defaming his reputation, he cared more for the workers and their families. Not only this, but Pope Kyrillos even organised other jobs for all these unemployed workers, a perfect example of displaying peace and unconditional love towards our enemies.

What the Fathers Say

Be instead of an avenger, a deliverer. Instead of an accuser, a peace maker

– St. Isaac the Syrian

REFLECTION

Why do I always get frustrated or agitated at even the smallest things? When my brother or sister upsets me, why do I become so filled with anger, fury and revenge? Look at the example of Isaac, who was treated with evil but insisted on keeping peace!

CHAPTER 27

JACOB VS ESAU

In chapter 27, we observe a significant conflict between Jacob and Esau which sets the scene for the next few chapters of the book. Isaac is ageing, and as per custom at the time, desired to bless his eldest son before he dies. So Isaac calls Esau and asks him to prepare a meal before he can receive the blessing. Overhearing this whole conversation is Rebekah, who devises a cunning plan to ensure that Jacob receives the blessing instead. When Isaac and Esau find out, they are deeply distressed and Esau vows revenge against Jacob immediately.

This whole story raises an interesting question: were Rebekah and Jacob wrong in going out and deliberately deceiving Isaac? The scholars say that if there was any deception, it was on the part of Isaac and Esau and NOT Rebekah and Jacob for two reasons:

1. During Rebekah's pregnancy, God revealed to her and Isaac that the younger twin would be the blessed one (Gen 25:23). This is no different to Isaac himself who as the younger sibling, was more blessed than Ishmael. With this knowledge, Isaac should have followed God's wishes and not ignored them. Also the blessing of the birthright was a huge ceremonial deed and should have been carried out in Rebekah's presence. The fact that Isaac went behind her back shows that it was in fact him being a little deceitful.

Events

CHAPTER 27

2.	Esau had sold his birthright-something Isaac would have known. By selling his birthright, Esau had entered a contract with his brother. If Esau was honest, he would have admitted this to his father. Hence Esau is the deceiver! Rebekah and Jacob were essentially justified in getting Jacob's rightful blessing! The proof of this is in the fact that God never rebuked Rebekah or Jacob for their actions. Later on, we will also see that Isaac never takes back the blessing once he realises it is Jacob that he blessed. He accepts what has happened as the right course of action.

Even though Rebekah and Jacob were justified in their decision, they should have chosen a more honest course of action. Rebekah could have simply faced Isaac with what she had overheard. Instead, she chose a more shrewd deed and this resulted in her being separated from Jacob for most of his life. Likewise, Jacob could have dealt with the scenario in a more honest manner and he received his due punishment, being forced

> **What the Fathers Say**
>
> Repentance is even capable of changing the adulterers into virgins.
>
> – The Desert Fathers

Birthright in the Old Testament

Just like Esau sold his birthright to Jacob two chapters ago, Esau misses out on receiving his father's blessing in this chapter, again at the expense of his brother Jacob. By selling his birthright, Esau basically sold the right to his blessing as well. But what exactly is this birthright which Esau sold? This word denotes the special privileges and advantages which belongs to the first-born son amongst any Jewish family. Essentially, he becomes the priest of the family, and is allocated a leadership role within the household. Further, whoever received the birthright was allotted double a portion of their paternal inheritance. However, this is an Old Testament concept, and now our birthright is being sons and daughters of our Lord Jesus Christ.

> **People, Places & Things**

to wait 14 years to marry Rachel (more about this later).

ESAU IS ANGRY

When Esau asks for the birthright, he describes himself to Isaac as 'your son, your firstborn, Esau' (verse 32). Esau had no right to say this because he gave away the right to be the firstborn two chapters ago. This means that it was in fact Jacob who was entitled to come and take the title of first born, explaining Isaac's response: 'Indeed he shall be blessed' (verse 33). In other words, Jacob was not to lose the blessing which he had received. This blessing was approved by God and would not be taken away. This is also confirmed by the fact that Isaac was not angry with Jacob, but was rather submissive to the events which had occurred.

In verse 34, Esau cried out: 'Bless me, me also, O my Father', but it was too late. Esau wasn't repentant over his actions. He was regretful. He was not sorry for what he had done, he was just sorry that he missed out on the blessing. This is cemented later on in the chapter when Esau reveals his intentions to kill Jacob once Isaac dies. In the same way, on the Day of Judgement, we will be forced to give an account for the things we regret and have not repented about. If Esau repented, the story would have ended up so differently, but Esau makes a simple mistake, doesn't repent and therefore suffers the consequences of his actions. It is not enough

What the Fathers Say

Even if you have lost hope in yourself, the Lord has not lost hope in your salvation. He has saved many, and you are not more difficult than all of them. When grace works in you, there is no room for despair. Enter into repentance with a courageous heart and do not belittle yourself

– Pope Shenouda III

to feel regret or sorrow over our sins, but we need to transform these feelings into genuine and true repentance. St. Peter denied Christ, regretted it and repented immediately. Meanwhile, Judas betrayed Christ, regretted it and instead of repenting, was led into despair.

THE REPENTANCE OF ST. PAES

A famous story of repentance is the story of St. Paes. She was not only a prostitute, but also the owner of a large brothel- leading a life which was extremely displeasing in the eyes of God. When St. John the Short heard about her, he approached her at the brothel, condemned her for her actions and taught her how to live a virtuous Christian life. Immediately, St. Paes left the brothel and went to the desert with St. John the Short. The next day St. Paes died and St. John the Short was worried over her salvation, whether or not her repentance was accepted. He then heard a voice from heaven saying: 'From the moment Paes left the brothel, her repentance was accepted'. This teaches us the importance of repentance and confession in wiping away all our sins.

REFLECTION

Is the fact that I am a son or daughter of Christ a source of continuous joy for me? Or do I take this privilege and honour for granted, just like Esau did with his birthright and blessings?

CHAPTER 28

Events

JACOB OBEYS, ESAU REBELS

Esau pledges to kill Jacob, and fearing for his life, Jacob flees at the advice of his mother Rebekah. This is a decision supported by Isaac, who doesn't send a servant to bring Jacob back a wife like Abraham did for him. Instead, Isaac sends Jacob away to find his own wife. Also, Isaac sends Jacob away with a blessing, further confirming that there is no anger on the part of Isaac towards Jacob. By blessing him, Isaac is confirming that what had happened is through the divine will of God.

When Jacob is fleeing, in verses 6-9 it is a further demonstration of the evil which has filled Esau's heart. After hearing Isaac's instructions to Jacob to 'not take a wife from the daughters of Canaan', Esau takes yet another unlawful wife as a sign of rebellion against his parents. Esau is in denial about the loss of his birthright, and vents out his frustration towards his parents. This highlights to us the danger of anger. What starts of a small seed of uncontrolled anger, can eventually become cursing, swearing, gossiping, rebellion and even a desire for murder (as was the case with Esau)! Therefore, we are instructed to 'Be angry and do not sin' (Ephesians 4: 26).

JACOB'S DREAM

From verse 10 onwards, Jacob begins his journey and he stops to rest along the way. While asleep, Jacob has a dream of a ladder on earth which reached up to heaven, with angels ascending and descending on it. The fathers have many contemplations on this dream. Even Jacob had his own interpretation, calling the place where he dreamt 'the house of God' (verse 17).

Most of the fathers agree that the stone is Christ. Recall Christ being described as 'the chief cornerstone' (Psalm 118:22). Jacob as a farmer always enjoyed a luxurious bed, but when he had nothing and no support, then God became his only supporter. In his father's house he had luxuries and never needed a stone. But when was on his own, he needed the comfort stone which is Christ. God reveals Himself to us when we are most in need, or when we have deprived ourselves of earthly luxuries and pleasures. When we are in comfort and fulfilling our earthly passions and pleasures, we don't see God. However, when we are abandoned by everyone, when we fast, when we deny our bodies of sin and pleasure, only then will we be made worthy to receive God's comfort and power.

What the Fathers Say

Remember that every single time you refuse to bow down to Satan and resist the pleasures and lusts of the body, God will send His angels to minister to you too

– Fr Yacoub Magdy

Jacob's Ladder: a symbol of our life on earth

Jacob's ladder resembled the connection between the earthly and the heavenly, and is symbolic of our relationship with God as well. There are many steps which one must take in order to build this relationship. God is already coming towards us, knocking on the door, but are we ready to approach Him in humility and zeal? If one of us is standing on the first step, let him not despair to reach the second one. And who stands on the second, let him not lose hope of reaching the third. How happy are those martyrs, many of whom were worthy of ascending to the ultimate steps, the top itself. Yet we too should not stop at the first step, but strive to ascend to higher steps.

People, Places &Things

What the Fathers Say

I believe that the Cross of the Saviour is the ladder seen by Jacob. On the ladder, the angels were seen ascending and descending. On the ladder, namely the Cross, the unrepentant were descending and the repentant were ascending.

— St. Jerome

Also, the ladder at the time was made of wood therefore representing the Cross of Christ. It is fixed to the ground and reaching up to heaven, meaning that it reconciles the heavenly with the earthly. The angels descending and ascending are carrying our prayers up to God. Finally, the Lord God is sitting above the ladder which represents the resurrection. This is because after the resurrection, the Lord Christ sat at the right hand of the Father as salvation became complete.

MORE ON THE LIBYAN MARTYRS

This chapter shows us how God walks with the humble, the needy and those being persecuted. There are many practical examples of this, including the recent story of the 21 Libyan martyrs, which we have already discussed. These men were asked to deny Christ or be killed. With confidence and without fear, they chose to be killed for the sake of their faith. A famous American psychologist analysed the video footage of their gruesome murder and concluded that these men must have had a mental or psychological impairment, or been given sedative drugs. There was simply no way they could remain so calm and composed even in the face of death! What the psychologist didn't know was that the martyrs were being aided by divine support, which could overcome even the greatest trials and tribulations!

REFLECTION

When I feel empty, lonely, anxious or sad, do I run to Christ to receive His divine comfort, just like Jacob did?

CHAPTER 29

JACOB MEETS RACHEL

In verses 1-12, Jacob encounters Rachel for the first time. At an event level, Jacob is eager to get on with his life because he feels that God is with him. This story reminds us of Isaac and how Rebekah came to be his wife. In both cases, a meeting happens at a well. Now at a deeper, spiritual level, we look for Christ in the story. The fathers see Jacob as representing Christ. He left his father's house to find a wife in the same way the Christ left his Father's house (heaven) to take the Church as His wife. Jacob meets Rachel at the well. Christ meets the Church at the well of Baptism because this is where our relationship with Him begins. After this, Jacob kissed Rachel. In a similar manner, the reconciliation between heaven and earth could only occur after our baptism.

Initially, Jacob agrees to work seven years to win Rachel's hand in marriage. We see how much he is willing to work in the name of love. In the exact same way, Christ was willing to accept so much suffering for His love of the Church. Recall John 3:16- 'For God so loved the world that He gave His only begotten Son that whoever believes in Him should not perish but have eternal life'. This famous verse is pretty much a summary of the entire gospel and teaches us the extent of God's love for us. The way Jacob loved Rachel is the same way which God loves His church. Notice the extent of Jacob's love. How he

Events

CHAPTER 29

worked for seven whole years but "they only seemed a few days to him"!

JACOB MARRIES LEAH AND RACHEL

When Jacob asks for Rachel's hand in marriage, Laban (her father) starts to display his true nature and he demands that Jacob works seven years to marry her. Then, in verses 21-30, Laban's deceit is further obvious. Instead of giving Rachel, he gives Leah and then demands that Jacob works another seven years if he wants Rachel. If he was an honest man, he would have disclosed beforehand that the younger daughter could not marry before the older. However, Laban's intentions were for personal gain and he used Jacob's love for Rachel against him.

On the night of Jacob's first marriage to Leah, many people would have been very upset. Rachel would have been silenced or banished by her father. Leah was uneasy with

What the Fathers Say

With love, nothing is difficult. Labour is easy to the one who longs for it

– St. Jerome

Love in the Ancient Culture

Jacob loved Rachel, and was willing to work seven years (and then another seven years!) to seek her hand in marriage. These seven years, without pay, seemed to pass as quickly as a few days. In this ancient culture, Jacob was not allowed to spend as much time as he wanted with Rachel. There were strict social guidelines to separate unmarried men and women. This demonstrates an important principle: true love waits. Jacob was willing to wait seven years for Rachel. In the same way, we should abide by the same principles, and be patient waiting on the Lord who knows our requirements even before we ask. In a time which is extremely sexualised, we may often use this as an excuse for ourselves. However, let us observe and learn from the example of our father Jacob who waited patiently and without haste.

People, Places &Things

What the Fathers Say

If you are in great troubles, fear, pain and sadness, and the enemy has been stalking you day and night, you shouldn't be afraid or scared. This is not the end. The happy end is coming, and the Lord will come. The Lord is sleeping just because you are, awake Him to rebuke the wind

– Fr Matthew the Poor

what she was doing to her sister. Jacob was displeased after being fooled by Laban. This shows us the domino effect of sin- Laban's greed not only impacted him, but three others as well. In a similar manner, our actions not only impact us, but our surroundings as well. In the words of Mother Teresa: 'You might be the only Bible which someone reads today'. Therefore, we must always take guard against sin, not just for our sakes, but for the sake of our brothers and sisters as well.

Jacob worked fourteen years with one goal: to marry Rachel. He worked the first seven years in fear of Laban, and was forced to marry Leah instead. The second seven years were worked in love, knowing that he would marry Rachel. Leah represents the fear of God, while Rachel represents His love. To reach the love of God, we must first have the fear of God. Even though prayer, Bible reading and church services are sometimes 'boring' and 'tiring', we must force ourselves to persist with them until God's grace eventually fills our heart and we will come to enjoy our time with the Lord.

THE MONK WHO DIDN'T ENJOY PRAYER

There is a famous story of a monk who always used to get bored and tired praying, especially before he slept. The devil would always tempt him to skip his night time prayers by making him lazy and complacent, putting many excuses in his mind like, 'you've had a long day', 'you already prayed this morning' and the list goes on. However, the monk would always tell himself: 'Imagine if you died tomorrow. How could you face God on Judgement Day without praying?'. It was this fear of God which forced the monk to pray regardless of these thoughts, and eventually God allowed him to enjoy prayer as well. If we are willing to exert so much effort and energy into our studies or into going to the gym for example, how much more should we work towards a relationship with our Lord and Saviour Jesus Christ.

REFLECTION

Observe the great love which Jacob had for Rachel, that seven years passed by like a matter of seconds! Do I have this love for God and if I don't, do I at least work and pray for this love?

CHAPTER 30

LEAH GIVES BIRTH, RACHEL IS BARREN

Events

CHAPTER 30

Moving on to chapter 30, Rachel is upset, She has seen her sister Leah bear four children, but she herself is still barren. It's been at least four years now, so Rachel would be feeling ashamed because marriage with no children at the time was shameful. She knew the problem lay with her because Jacob had already fathered four children. Rachel is no longer satisfied with the love of her husband-she needs to be a mother. This is why Jacob is angry towards her. Jacob worked fourteen years to marry her and now she is not satisfied with him.

Jacob chose Rachel first but God chose Leah to bear children first, showing that God works in mysterious ways. Rachel was the beloved one but Leah was the blessed one. Leah never envied Rachel. Instead, she put her hope in God. However, Rachel envied Leah. The one who was beautiful on the outside was not beautiful on the inside. Rachel's barrenness leads her to ask her maid Bilhah to bear her a son with Jacob instead (verses 3-6). She was willing to accept the son of a maid as her son more than she was willing to accept her sister's son as her own. This was not a healthy situation. Rachel is willing to share her marriage with another woman just so she can have a child! Unlike Sarah who was saddened because Abraham didn't have any children, Rachel is driven by self-interest only. She is pushed by envy and is aiming to get back at her sister.

THE JEALOUSY CONTINUES

Unfortunately in verses 9-13, Leah is unhappy because she has now stopped giving birth. She mimics Rachel's behaviour and gives Jacob her maid Zilpah to have children by her. By doing this, she allows herself to be dragged into her sister's anger and envy. Just because Leah no longer bore any children, this didn't mean that Jacob stopped seeing her, so there was no need for Leah to go down this path. Furthermore, Leah already had four children. Leah simply stopped being thankful. Envy and jealousy had destroyed the spirituality and love between the two sisters. This is what happens when we stopped being thankful.

GIVING THANKS

The importance of thanksgiving should not be undermined in our lives. Rachel and Leah were driven by jealousy and envy, and both refused to acknowledge the gifts

What the Fathers Say

Jealousy has no limit; it is an evil that continually endures and a sin without end. The lies of jealousy burn hotter in proportion to the increasing success of the person who is envied

— St. Cyprian of Carthage

Jacob's Odd Breeding Program

Jacob desires to leave from the presence of Laban, and demands his rightful wages. But what he asks for is rather strange. He asks for every speckled and spotted sheep, every black lamb and every spotted and speckled goat. This initially seemed like a good deal for Laban, since his flock of sheep mainly consisted of pure white sheep. However, Jacob does something extremely strange here, he takes fresh cut branches of poplar, almond and plane trees, and places them in the water which the flock of sheep were to drink. Somehow, this led to an increase in the number of spotted sheep who were born. The Bible does not explain or give any logical explanation to this, but we can attribute this increase in providence to God's blessing in Jacob's life.

People, Places &Things

which God bestowed upon them. Instead of thanking God, they decided to question God and take matters into their own hands. In our church services, we begin each of them with the thanksgiving prayers, whether this be the liturgy, marriages, Agpeya prayers or even funerals! There is no gift without increase except the gift without thanksgiving, and therefore thanksgiving should form a fundamental part of each of our prayers.

There is a famous story about a holy priest from one of the churches in Egypt. St. Mary appeared to this priest and asked him if he was in need of anything or had any particular requests for God. The priest replied to St. Mary: 'Tell your Son I am in need of nothing'. This shows that he was completely satisfied with everything he had! It is this virtue of thanksgiving which pleases the heart of God and inclines God to bestow upon us even more blessings!

REFLECTION

Why is my prayer always filled with requests and demands on God? Let's learn to start off every prayer by giving thanks, and showing our Father that we appreciate all He has given us!

CHAPTER 31

JACOB LEAVES LABAN

In this chapter, God orders Jacob to leave Laban. Jacob speaks to his wives in a wise and rational manner, explaining the situation and his dream (verse 10). They see their father's deception and immoral behaviour so they agree with everything Jacob says and agree to leave. They also see how God is working with Jacob and are now on Jacob's side. It is important to notice that Laban's deception was not a one-off thing: not only did he force Jacob to work 14 years for Rachel, but he also cheated him and changed his wage ten times (verse 41).

In verses 17-24, Jacob is a symbol of Christ who came into the world, laboured tirelessly, married the Church and then went back to His Father. Meanwhile, Laban represents Satan. Jacob took Leah and Rachel (who used to be the possession of Laban i.e. Satan) and made them His own. In the same way, Christ took humanity from the authority of the devil and married the church through His love. And just as Satan didn't recognise that Christ was the Son of God till He resurrected on the third day, so too Laban didn't notice that Jacob had fled till the third day (verse 22). Even after finding out that Jacob ran away, Laban still dared to chase after him to bring back what was taken from him. This is the exact same fight we have with Satan today. He is fighting humanity, you and me, to try and keep us from making it to the Heavenly Father.

Events

CHAPTER 31

THE BATTLE BETWEEN GOD AND SATAN

Satan never gives up. But just as God told Laban: 'Be careful that you speak to Jacob neither good nor bad' (verse 24), likewise Satan can't touch us. We are no longer under his authority, for we have been redeemed by Christ's blood on the Cross. In the life of St. Anthony, several of his encounters with the devil are recounted. The devil would appear to him in the form of serpents, scorpions and many other wild beasts, attempting to destroy Him. However, St. Anthony would reply: 'If there had been any power in you, it would have sufficed had one of you come, but since the Lord has made you weak you attempt to terrify me by numbers'. This shows us the God-given authority we have over Satan.

Satan has no authority over us, and even if he causes us to sin, we can repent and sing:

The Covenant: a Pillar of Stones

Laban wisely asks for a covenant to be made between him and Jacob, so that neither of them would harm the other. Jacob took a stone and set it as a pillar; and they made a heap of stones, and they ate on the heap for the sake of reconciliation. That heap of stones was called 'Jegar Shadutha' in Syrian by Laban, and 'Galeed' in Hebrew by Jacob. Both names mean "the heap of testimony" or "the watch tower". It is as if God would be watching over them.

They also broke bread and shared it together, and were of the same blood. Now what exactly does this all resemble? This pillar refers to none other than the Cross of our Lord Jesus Christ, lifted up on the Mount of Calvary, which would become the pillar and cornerstone of our faith, protecting us from all evil. Further, Christ offered us His own body and blood on the Cross, and this is a testimony to the truth of reconciliation!

People, Places &Things

"Do not rejoice over me, my enemy. For when I fall, I will arise. When I sit in darkness, the Lord will be a light to me" (Malachi 7:8). For man was made for God, and God is always waiting patiently for us to return in order to provide us with blessings and His true divine joy.

LABAN ENCOUNTERS JACOB

When Laban hears that Jacob has fled from him, he is infuriated and pursues him immediately. Laban has bad intentions towards him and quite possibly desired to harm him- hence God's apparition in verse 24. And even though Jacob had a three day head start, Laban still caught up, showing his evil intentions and genuine intention (determination?) to inflict harm.

But this raises an interesting question: if Laban was evil, why would God appear to him? In the Old Testament, God appeared not only to the righteous people, but also to the wicked ones to prevent them from carrying out their evil deeds. The appearance of God is very clear since it curbed the anger of Laban and stopped him from harming Jacob. This shows us how much God looks after His people. He will condescend and appear to evil people to protect His righteous children. We may not see God, but He is working all the time to protect us from both hidden and visible trials and temptations. And God is even willing to appear and intervene with evil men in order to protect us from the attacks of the adversary!

WHO STOLE THE FALSE GODS?

In verse 30, Laban accuses Jacob of stealing his gods. Jacob replies that he has not stolen the gods, and that whoever has stolen them shall surely die (he did not yet know that it was in fact his wife Rachel who had taken them). Rachel hid these gods with the other gods she used to worship, and because of this, she died in childbirth before she reached Canaan. She had broken one of the Ten Commandments: 'You shall have no other gods beside Me' (Exodus 20:3).

Note that God did not allow Laban to discover who had stolen the gods because he wanted to give Rachel a chance to repent. God knows everything that we do and is waiting for us to repent and confess. It is only when we don't do this, that we will be judged. On judgement day, God won't ask us why we sinned, He will ask us why we didn't repent. Now since Rachel didn't repent, the judgement came upon her and she died before reaching Canaan. God will often cover our sins to avoid exposing or embarrassing us, but we should never take advantage of this mercy and love- we must confess to our spiritual father and repent before God in order to be forgiven. There is no sin without forgiveness except the sin which is without repentance- therefore, let us learn from the

> ## What the Fathers Say
>
> *Do not despair. For in God's mercy, even after we fall into sin, He is capable of elevating us to into an even higher spiritual state than we were before the fall*
>
> *– Fr Yacoub Magdy*

example of Rachel and repent while we have the opportunity to do so.

REFLECTION

God has protected us from many problems that we knew were coming our way, and other problems which we were not even aware of! Do I remember to thank God for this divine protection every day?

CHAPTER 32

Events

CHAPTER 32

JACOB PREPARES TO MEET ESAU

After meeting Laban and finally making peace with him, Jacob then prepares to meet Esau and make peace as well. In verses 1-2, Jacob is met by the angels of God. Jacob knew that he was in the presence of angels, but we don't know how. However, it wasn't just a vision- it was an actual physical meeting. This means that there was an important message from God which was delivered to him. God is basically telling Jacob: 'Do not be afraid. I am with you'.

When giving instructions to his messengers, Jacob refers to Esau as his 'lord' and himself as the 'servant' (verse 4). Jacob has peace in his heart and as such speaks calmly and peacefully to his brother. However, Esau's response was not peaceful (verses 6-8). Jacob was afraid. His inner peace did not last for very long. When God gives us His reassurance, the obstacles of the world should not shake our faith in His promises. Even though Jacob saw an army of angels which could have easily conquered Esau's 400 men, he was still scared.

In verses 9-12, Jacob makes an extremely humble prayer to the Lord God. He begins by addressing Him as the 'God of my father Abraham'. In a similar manner, he taught us to pray by crying out 'Our Father'. He then humbles himself and considers himself 'unworthy of the least of all mercies' which God has bestowed upon Him, before moving on to his request for God's protection. Observe the sequence of this prayer! He calls out to God His Father, giving thanks first before finally putting his request in front of God. In a like manner, we must always begin our prayer with thanksgiving, because, by looking around us, we will find hundreds of reasons to be grateful to God, whether this be family, friends, food, education and even the chance to be alive and repent!

JACOB WRESTLES WITH GOD: A LIFE-CHANGING EVENT

Towards the end of this chapter, one of the most intriguing encounters of the Bible takes place. Jacob wrestles with God. Until now, there are many unanswered questions about this passage. Some scholars believe that Jacob wrestled with an angel because they were uncomfortable with the concept of the appearance of the Logos in the Old Testament. However, the Bible says 'Man' in verse 24 and not angel, hence we believe that this is incorrect.

In his dream in chapter 28, Jacob saw the angels and the Lord. However, as the years passed by, Jacob is now considered worthy of meeting the Lord face to face and even wrestling with Him. For Jacob, this was a life-changing event which transformed his life forever. But why does God wrestle Jacob? God saw that Jacob was afraid of Esau and he was praying for a solution. So God appeared to Jacob and began wrestling with him (not

What the Fathers Say

Why did Jacob wrestle with God and catch him? Because "the Kingdom of Heaven suffers violence, and the violent take it by force" (Mat 11:12). Why did He wrestle? In order to get him by labour, as whatever we get after strife, we hold onto more firmly

– St. Augustine

fighting!). This represents a significant trial or tribulation, almost a crisis in the life of Jacob. He is all alone, terrified in fear from his brother, and now he is wrestling with a stranger (at this stage he does not know that this is in fact God!) in the middle of the desert! But God allows Jacob to face this trial to transform and change his life, and instead of escaping or shying away from it, Jacob fights with God "until the breaking of day" (i.e. a very long time).

Jacob is committed to wrestling with God and does not shy away. Instead, he embraces the challenge, holds on to God and exclaims in verse 26: "I will not let You go unless You bless me!". This is the perfect and ideal response for anyone facing hardship; clinging on to God and refusing to let him go! God then asks Jacob: "what is your name?", a seemingly strange question given the circumstances. However, the word "Jacob" in Hebrew means deceiver, so essentially, God is asking Jacob to admit his weakness and acknowledge that huge flaw that needs to be changed in his personality. It is as if Jacob is admitting to

People, Places &Things

Gid Hanasheh: the sciatic nerve

The term *Gid Hanasheh* in Hebrew is often translated as "displaced tendon", and is the term for sciatic nerve in Judaism. The sciatic nerve is a large nerve in humans and animals which branches from the lower back, through to the hips and buttocks and down each leg. According to Jewish tradition, Israelites do not ea the thigh muscle which is ove the hip, because of their belie that the "angel of God" (w believe that this was in fac the "Son of God") touche and displaced Jacob's hi socket whilst wrestling wit God (Genesis 32:32).

all the deception he has committed in his life, from stealing Esau's birthright, then stealing Esau's blessing and even deceiving his father-in-law Laban too! God observing his honest confession and zeal for change responds: "Your name shall no longer be called Jacob, but Israel" (verse 28). And "Israel" means "the prince of God", which means that God has accepted Jacob's yearning for change and transformed him into a prince!

Do you too desire to be changed? Are you tired or feeling anxious or depressed, repeating the exact same sin over and over again, or constantly doubting God? Everyone wants to change. The first step, just like Jacob, is to acknowledge the problem or crisis in your life. Instead of escaping it, learn to embrace the challenge and be persistent in your battle to overcome it. This means to pray with zeal and fervour to overcome your problem and to tell God: "I will not leave You till You bless me", just like Jacob did! This also involves admitting and acknowledging there is a problem, and confessing it, just like Jacob did when he admitted to his deception and answered God's question: "what is your name?". Confess the sin or weakness to yourself, confess it to your spiritual guide/ confession father and most importantly, confess it to God. Then God will provide you with his mercy and grace, and you too will be able to change your life and become a "prince of God", just like Jacob was!

What the Fathers Say

It is hard for a man to find strength in his tribulations without a gift from God which is received through the ardent pursuit of prayer and the outpouring of repentant tears

– St. Isaac the Syrian

DISLOCATING JACOB'S HIP

When the Lord didn't prevail against Jacob, he touched his hip socket (verse 25). He didn't hit or punch it- but still managed to dislocate it. This was a supernatural touch because with a mere touch God can dislocate a hip? God left Jacob with a sign of weakness to remind Him to completely rely on God and not on his own human strength.

Many people only come to God when they hit rock bottom in their lives. After all avenues have been extinguished and they have not found the satisfaction and support that they desire, then as a last resort they think of God. But even these people were saved. Jesus speaks a parable (in Matthew 20) in which he teaches us that those of the eleventh hour received the same wage as those of the first hour. It's not too late to come to God and ask for His mercy. Today, we should come to God and bring him all our weaknesses, knowing that He is greater than them all!

REFLECTION

Do we expect our Christian life to be simple and effortless? Does anything worth having come without effort? How do we take the Kingdom of Heaven by force in our lives? Do we always choose to take the narrow path, fighting to stay on it, or quickly succumb to our weakness, forgetting God's strength?

CHAPTER 33

CHAPTER 33

Events

JACOB FINALLY MEETS ESAU

After all the build-up, Jacob and Esau finally meet and reconcile after many years apart. Notice that Jacob displays no fear rather, he is full of inner peace and respect towards his long-lost brother. Jacob presented himself ahead of the rest of his family, showing that he was willing to be killed for them. This shows how much Jacob loves his family. In the same way, Christ presented Himself to the Father, taking the blame for all our sins, even though he Himself was blameless.

Verse 4 is very similar to the story of the Prodigal son. Just like the father waited outside the gate for his son, bowing down and embracing him upon return, so too does Esau run towards Jacob, bowing down and kissing him. This teaches us a very important lesson, that God can speak to the heart of our enemies if we remain humble. Jacob harboured no hatred in his heart towards Esau, and as such, God was able to soften Esau's heart towards him. Even though Esau felt extreme resentment towards Jacob for stealing both his blessing and birthright, even to the extent of wanting to kill Jacob only a few chapters ago, these ill feelings have now disappeared!

THE POWER OF FORGIVENESS

There is a very famous story in America of a serial killer by the name of Gary Ridgway, who was convicted of 48 separate murder counts. In his court appearance, the parents of all those whom he had killed began to curse and swear at him, wishing that he 'burn in hell', 'suffer for his actions' and even 'be killed for them'. He stood there, emotionless and unaffected by all the hate that he was receiving. One man (whose daughter had been murdered by Gary) stood up and said: 'There are people here that hate you. I'm not one of them. You've made it difficult to live up to what I believe and that is what God says to do, to forgive. You are forgiven sir'. With this, the seemingly emotionless Gary burst into tears, unable to comprehend the love and forgiveness of this old man. This is a powerful story which teaches us how loving our enemies will allow God to work wonders in both our and their lives. This touching video can be found on YouTube, and has inspired many to understand the power of forgiveness.

What the Fathers Say

If you have nothing to give people, give them a warm smile and a kind word. Give them love, give them tenderness. Give them a kind word, give them encouragement

– Pope Shenouda III

Offering of Gifts: a Symbol of Peace

Jacob is initially terrified to meet his brother Esau and must have been fearing for his life at first. However, he was unaware that God had already moved the heart of Esau, who instead became filled with love and compassion towards his younger brother. In an attempt to appease Esau's expected anger, Jacob had prepared many generous gifts for Esau. However, Esau initially refuses, claiming: "I have enough", indicating that he harbours no ill feeling towards his brother and has acquired inner peace. However, Jacob urges Esau and he eventually accepts them. The acceptance of these gifts is significant. In ancient Jewish culture, one never accepted a gift from an enemy, only a friend. To accept the gifts meant to accept the friendship, indicating that forgiveness was ultimately achieved!

People, Places &Things

JACOB GIVES HIS WEALTH TO ESAU

After Jacob meets Esau, he offers him a significant portion of his wealth. Esau refuses initially, but Jacob is adamant that Esau receives the gift. Only the day before, Jacob had seen God face to face, so materialistic wealth means nothing to him anymore. Jacob is happy to give away his possessions, given that he has received the greatest gift of all: seeing God. Once we encounter God's love and Fatherhood, everything else in the world becomes so small in comparison!

Giving comes at two levels: the giving which we force ourselves to do, and the giving which we do with great joy. You may start by giving the 10% of your possessions (time, money etc.) but the more your love for God grows, the more you will learn to give unconditionally and joyfully. We see how much Jacob is willing to give after his encounter with God. Previously all he wanted was to take. It is an honour and great blessing to learn to give with joy, to give in abundance and to give without counting.

In verses 18-20, Jacob arrives peacefully in the city of Shechem. He buys some land and builds an altar which he calls 'God the God of Israel' (El Elohe Israel). He does not use his old name of Jacob, but rather his new name Israel. This signifies a new beginning. The night Jacob wrestled with God became the turning point in his life, and this gave him strength and the ability to overcome

> The rite of mutual forgiveness is far from being just a ritual. It can be, and often is, a profoundly effective event which changes the life of both the one who forgives and he who is forgiven.
>
> — Bishop Kallistos of Diokleia

all his weaknesses. When we allow God to take control of our lives, regardless of any hardships we face, we can trust that He will allow us to overcome them all. This concept was described by St. Paul when God informed him that "My grace is sufficient for you, for my strength is made perfect in weakness" (2 Cor 12:9).

REFLECTION

Am I still harbouring anger, hatred or ill-feelings towards someone who has wronged me in the past? Today is the day to let go, just like God has forgiven me unconditionally, I too should forgive my brethren for their sins!

CHAPTER 34

Events

CHAPTER 34

THE DINAH INCIDENT

This chapter recounts a unique story which attracted very little attention from our church fathers. Dinah, the only daughter of Jacob, left her house and went to make friends with the other girls in the land. She was noticed by Shechem, the prince of the land, who immediately felt an attraction to her. As a young man, he was driven by his passion and forced himself upon her, laying in bed with her. However, the custom of the time was to ask the father for permission before approaching their daughter. This meant that Shechem not only defiled Dinah, but Dinah's entire family by not following the laws of the time.

Throughout this whole matter, Jacob kept silent. However, Jacob's sons decided to take matters into their own hands. When Shechem's father approached Jacob's family to apologise, Jacob's sons insisted that Shechem's whole family be circumcised to correct the mistake. Of course, this was completely unacceptable because the purpose of circumcision had nothing to do with marriage. Circumcision was a covenant between God and the people of Israel. Jacob's sons were using a sacred religious deed for their own revenge. They are turning something Godly and holy into an act of revenge.

Shechem and his father accept the conditions- but unfortunately they do not agree to be circumcised for the original reason circumcision was intended, but rather to please and quieten Jacob's sons. We sometimes do the same and follow God's commandments to please man, rather than to please God. Sometimes we go to church on Sundays just because everyone else does it. Sometimes we act righteous and holy in front of people only so we can win their praise. But remember, everyone who is praised by man loses the praise of God. Therefore, we must follow the commandments of God to build our own personal relationship with him alone.

THE CONSEQUENCES OF IMPURITY

This whole story started with one impure desire which stemmed from the heart of Shechem. Shechem looked at Dinah, loved her, lusted for her and then violated her. Notice the consequences:

1. All his family had to be circumcised (defiling the covenant of God).

What the Fathers Say

The goal of our profession is to reach the kingdom of God. Its immediate purpose however, is the purity of heart, for without it we cannot reach our goal

— St. Moses the Strong

Homar and Shechem

After Shechem's grave mistake of violating Dinah, Shechem's father, Homar, decides to take matters into his own hands by apologising to the family on his behalf and agreeing to circumcise all his people to keep the peace. If Shechem means "shoulder" and Homar is derived from "homar" (Arabic) or "donkey", what Shechem and his father did resembles the work of the devil, who persuades creatures to be defiant towards God and behave according to carnal thought, just like a donkey. The devil corrupts and violates the human soul, to get it corrupted like Dinah, by stubborn and persistent lustful thoughts which can eventually destroy the human soul. Thus, this confirms the words of St. Paul who asked: 'What communion has light with darkness' (2 Cor 6:14).

People, Places &Things

Show the Lord loyalty and refuse the sinful joy of the world, that is pornography and sexual sins, and rest assured that you will instead experience the divine joy which comes from God

– Fr. Yacoub Magdy

2. All his family were murdered. None of them were spared.

This shows us the consequences of lust and impurity, not only on the individual, but also on their family and whole community. What may start as a simple, innocent glance or search on the internet could end up destroying someone's life. The sin of adultery and lust is despised by God, and He reminds us that whoever sows of his flesh will of the flesh reap corruption. Therefore, if any of us have a problem with lust, pornography or any similar sin, it must stop today, because neither fornicators, nor adulterers, nor homosexuals will enter the kingdom of heaven (1 Cor 6:9). And who are those who commit adultery? Whoever looks at a woman with lust has already committed adultery with her in his heart (Mat 5: 28).

Even though God's punishment is harsh, He is more than willing to accept our repentance and confession and He promised us that 'as far as the east is from the west', He will separate our sins from us (Psalm 103: 2). This is shown in the story of St. Mary the Egyptian. She was a prostitute from her youth, unable to control the desires of her body. One day she saw crowds of people on a ship, travelling towards Jerusalem to celebrate the feast of the Cross. She decided to join them, even committing fornication on the ship due to her uncontrollable desire. Upon arriving in Jerusalem, she tried to enter the church but was 'drawn back by some kind of force'. No matter how hard she tried, she was not able to enter- even though those around her seemed to enter with ease. She immediately realised this was because of her sin and begged the Virgin Mary to pray for her forgiveness. St. Mary appeared to her in a vision and instructed her to live in the desert, where she lived for many years. After St. Zosima gave her Holy Communion, Mary prayed 'Lord now You are letting Your servant depart in peace according to Your word' and departed to heaven. This story teaches us that we too can overcome the lusts and desires of our bodies and should not despair, regardless of our spiritual state.

REFLECTION

Do I try my absolute best to ensure that I keep my purity before the Lord? Or do I fall into the same sexual mistakes that the rest of the world does, knowing that this deeply displeases the heart of God?

CHAPTER 35

GENESIS FOR TEENS

GOD PROTECTS JACOB

After Simeon and Levi killed all the family of Shechem, Jacob fears retaliation from their neighbouring inhabitants. Jacob was previously afraid of his brother Esau and God saved Him. Jacob was also afraid of his uncle Laban and again, God saved Him. This time is no different and once again God will show Jacob that He is with him in all his troubles. Therefore, in verse 5 we read that "the terror of God was upon the cities". Like before, Jacob was afraid but God turns around this to put fear into the hearts of those who were pursuing Jacob.

This shows us the loving nature of God who protects all His children from both hidden and visible problems. Our unrighteousness does not stop God's faithfulness towards us. God made a promise with Abraham that his descendants would be as the sand of the sea, and God made sure that this promise was kept regardless of Jacob's mistakes. Also, our fear of God puts fear in people because they become in awe of our fear of God. Even the Jews feared Christ- He appeared weak to them, but they still feared Him. Place Your life in God's hands and He will protect You from every single problem.

There are several promises in the Bible which teach us the gifts and blessings which come as a result of fearing God. Perhaps the most famous of these comes in Psalm 34: "The angel of the Lord encamps around those who fear him and delivers them" (verse 7) and "There is no want to those who fear Him. The young lions lack and suffer hunger, but those who fear the Lord will not lack any good thing" (verses 9 and 10). Here is a divine promise from the mouth of God- if you fear God, you will be in need of nothing! But how can we fear God? The answer is simple and twofold. Firstly, we must spend as much time with Him as possible. This could be prayer, Bible reading, enjoying the sacraments, service etc. Secondly, we must follow His commandments to the very best of our ability! This means resisting the devil as much as we physically can. By finding pleasure with God, we will never need to find or seek any pleasure within the world.

JACOB RETURNS 'HOME'

In verse 2, God sends Jacob back to the original place where he saw the ladder in his dreams, called 'the house of God' (verse 28). It has been about thirty years since this incident and God is reminding Jacob of the covenant He made with him. The fathers believe that about ten years have passed since Jacob left his uncle Laban, so it has taken him 10 years to move around this small area of Judea. We don't know why Jacob took so long, but God is now telling him it's about time you finally decided to come home. When we are in distress we run to God, but when matters settle down we slow and become complacent. It was only supposed to be an overnight trip, but Jacob took ten years with

> **What the Fathers Say**
>
> I have seen sin and corruption. I have left it and flee far away. I will abide in the desert and I shall see my God
>
> – St. Mina of Bayad

many stops on the way. However, when tribulations came his way, Jacob began to move again. This shows us that sometimes God allows trials and tribulations in our lives so that we may grow closer to Him.

Jacob is a spiritual person and in verses 2 and 3, he asks his household to do two things: "Get rid of the foreign gods among you" and "purify yourself and change your garments". These are two lessons which teach us how to return back to God and repent after being far away from him.

1. "Put away all foreign gods among you": this represents the sanctification of the soul. We cannot serve two masters, so we must separate ourselves from anything that has a hold on us, - love of fame, ego, social

People, Places &Things

The Birth of Benjamin

No doubt Rachel's heart was aching to give birth to a brother for Joseph, her firstborn and only child at the time. This desire was eventually fulfilled, and as they journeyed from Bethel, Rachel travailed in childbirth and she had hard labour. And so it was, as her soul was departing (for she died), she called his name "Ben-Oni", meaning "son of my grief" because of the pain and agony which she was enduring. However, his father called him Benjamin, meaning "son of my right hand". Now here raises a question. Why did God allow for Rachel's death as she delivered Him? Firstly, God wished to confirm to man that birth and death in human life go hand in hand, and that we will experience both joy and grief whilst in our mortal flesh. Secondly, Rachel represents the Church of the Gentiles, whilst Jacob is a symbol for Christ. The church must suffer and experience grief – "Ben-Oni" before they can experience the joy of fellowship at the right hand of Christ- "Benjamin".

status, money or even friends who have a negative impact on our life. Recall the story of the rich young ruler (Mat 19: 16-30) who kept every single commandment, but was sorrowful when Christ asked Him to sell all his possessions and follow Him. This man could not inherit the kingdom of heaven because his heart was too attached to something other than God.

2. "Purify yourself and change your garments": this represents the sanctification of the body and overcoming the desires of the flesh. Unfortunately, sexual sins such as pornography, masturbation and fornication have become normalised in today's society, but we must remember that only the pure in heart can see God. If we are struggling to witness the work of God in our lives, maybe this could be due to our own lack of purity!

THE ROPE ANALOGY

This chapter concludes rather uneventfully with the death of both Isaac (Jacob's father) and Rachel (Jacob's second wife). However, just a quick remark on the first point above. Just like Jacob we must instructed his household to "put away all foreign gods", we too must make this an absolute priority in our lives- to seek God more and focus less on earthly things. There was a famous preacher who used an extremely interesting rope analogy. Imagine holding a rope which goes on and on forever and ever. Now imagine that this rope resembled our

> **What the Fathers Say**
>
> *Everything in this world will perish very, very soon. Then what shall remain? God and God alone*
>
> *– Pope Shenouda III*

existence. The small tip of that rope would resemble our life here on earth, and the rest of the rope (which was infinite!) would resemble our eternal life. Most people spend all their life here on earth trying to enjoy that small tip of the rope- indulging in riches, falling into sin, enjoying sexual pleasures and even studying and working hard to enjoy a successful future. But there's a problem; what we do in this life on earth (that tiny tip of the rope), determines where we will spend the rest of our eternity (the infinite part of the rope). Therefore, we should always remember "to seek first the kingdom of God and His righteousness, and all these things shall be added to you". (Mat 6:33) If the main purpose of our life here on earth is something other than a relationship with Christ, we need to repent and re-evaluate ourselves. Our lives on earth are just a preparation for an eternal life with God. We mention this during every liturgy, when the Priest prays: "we too who are sojourners in this world, keep us in your faith".

REFLECTION

Jacob instructed his people to "put away all the foreign gods among you". Are there any foreign gods, e.g. sins, pleasures, occupations, desires or anything else which I have prioritised in my life above God?

CHAPTER 36

Esau's descendants: Lessons to be learnt

Chapter 36 is simply a list of all the descendants of Esau. While these may just appear to be a bunch of names with little spiritual meaning or lessons to be learnt, everything in the Bible has a purpose. Firstly, this provides historical evidence to anyone that may have questions or doubts regarding the validity and authenticity of the Bible. More importantly, a certain priest made an extremely beautiful contemplation: "whenever we see a list of names written in the Bible, we too should pray to God that our names may also be written in the book of life!"

Events

CHAPTER 36

CHAPTER 37

Events

CHAPTER 37

ALL ABOUT JOSEPH!

Notice that in chapter 37, Joseph is the first person mentioned, even though he is son number 11. This demonstrates the importance of Joseph as a symbol of the Lord Jesus Himself. Joseph in the Old Testament was a type of Christ in the New Testament. Just like Christ was a Saviour to all mankind, so too was Joseph a saviour to the Jews during the famine that plagued the world (more about that later!). Therefore, the author does not follow the order of mentioning the firstborn. Joseph is the focus because he is a type of the Lord Jesus Christ Himself.

JOSEPH VS HIS BROTHERS

There is some obvious conflict between Joseph and his brothers. This is because Joseph is Jacob's first son from his favourite wife, Rachel. Therefore, Joseph is the favourite child, the spoiled one, and this creates tension between Joseph and his brothers. In verses 3-4, the situation is aggravated when Jacob gives Joseph the coloured tunic. Then, in verses 5-8, Joseph has a dream which he goes and tells his brothers. In his dream, all his brothers bowed down to him. He has another similar dream in verses 9-11, and once again boasts about it to his brothers. This is a sign of Joseph's naivety and lack of wisdom. If he knew that his brothers already hated him, why would he anger them even more? Even if the dream was from God, he should not have boasted about it. When God gives us a sign or speaks to us, we should keep it in our heart instead of sharing it or revealing it to others.

In verses 14-17, Joseph is keen to find his brothers and inquire of their wellbeing. He didn't give up until he found his brothers, even though he knew they hated him. He was eager to make sure they were well. This again is symbolic of Christ, who wandered around the world performing miracles, healing the sick and preaching. Just like Joseph searched for his brothers, Christ too searches for us and will not rest till he finds us.

In the famous icon of Christ standing at the door and knocking, notice that the door knob is only on the inside of the door, rather than the outside. This is because only we can open the door. Jesus is knocking, standing and waiting patiently, but we have to accept Him into our lives through prayer, Bible reading and the sacraments. This is a great message of hope! Again in the story of the prodigal son (Luke 15), the father was standing outside his

What the Fathers Say

Jacob sent his son to proclaim his worry for their safety; and God the Father sent His only-begotten Son to visit mankind, who were weak with sin, a lost flock. As Joseph sought his brothers, He wandered in the wilderness, and the Lord Christ, as He sought mankind, He wandered in the world
– Fr. Caesarius of Arles

The Tunic of Many Colours

Jacob, having loved Joseph more than all his brothers, made him a tunic of many colours. What is this coloured tunic but the Church of many nations, received by the Lord Christ from the hands of His Father as a price of His love for humanity? In Christ's transfiguration, "His clothes became as white as the light" (Mat 17:2), a reference to the Church which reflects the light of Christ. It is one tunic of many colours; thus, if one colour is removed, it would lose its beauty. In a similar manner, the Church proclaims its need for every single one of its members, whatever his colour, position, work or capacity.

People, Places &Things

What the Fathers Say

Joseph was taken to Egypt, and Christ came down to the world! Joseph saved Egypt from famine, and Christ freed the world from the famine to the word of God! If Joseph was not sold by his brothers, Egypt would not have been saved. And indeed, if the Jews did not crucify Christ, the world would have perished

- Fr. Caesarius of Arles

house for week after week, waiting for his son to return. When he finally returned, instead of being angry or upset with his son, he ran to him, bowed down before him, hugged him and then threw him a huge celebration. This shows us the beautiful humility of Christ who even bows down to us while we are sinners and is willing to accept even the worst amongst us.

THROWING JOSEPH INTO THE PIT

In verses 18-20, Joseph's brothers see him approaching and conspire to kill him. This is symbolic of the Jews conspiring to kill Christ. After eventually compromising their decision and instead throwing Joseph into the pit, the brothers sit to eat a meal. This also has special symbolism! It is the same as the Jews who were eager to crucify Christ before sitting down to eat the Passover meal. And just like Jesus was sold for 30 pieces of silver and He took the form of a slave, so too was Joseph sold to be a slave by his brothers for only 20 shekels - yet another similarity! There are many more lessons which can be learnt from the life of Joseph and many more attributes which make Him a type of the Lord Christ Himself.

REFLECTION

Just like Joseph's brothers were jealous of him, do I often look at the possessions of others and become filled with envy and spite too?

CHAPTER 38

CHAPTER 38

Events

WALKING, STANDING AND SITTING

Chapter 38 is not the natural continuation of chapter 37. The story of Joseph continues in chapter 39. However, Moses takes a side-track and brings up Judah in this chapter. This is the only chapter which discusses one of Jacob's other sons besides Joseph. The scholars believe that this chapter is evidence that the whole Old Testament is inspired by the Holy Spirit with one aim, Jesus Christ, and anything that is related to Him is mentioned. From the line of Judah the Messiah will come, therefore chapter 38 is all about Judah.

It appears that Judah was not happy with what his brothers did to Joseph, and he moved away to a smaller town to separate himself from this injustice. He married a Canaanite lady (which was unlawful for a Jewish man at the time) and remained in the area- mingling and interacting with people of the land. This was Judah's first mistake, keeping company with the sinners. We pray Psalm 1 in the Agpeya every day and it begins with "Blessed is the man who walks not in the counsel of the ungodly. Nor stands in the path of sinners. Nor sits in the seat of the scornful" (verses 1, 2). Notice the natural progression from "walks" to "stands" to "sits". Walking with sin is bad enough, but at least when we walk with sinners we have the choice to walk away. Once we stand with sinners, it is slightly harder and eventually, when we sit with sinners, it becomes very difficult to distance ourselves from the sin. That's why it's so important for us to cut sin off from its roots, whether that be gossiping, judging or sexual sins amongst many other things. Once we start sinning, it eventually becomes a habit which is difficult to resist. If I am hanging around the wrong group of friends, I should walk away before I become so attached to them and fall into even worse sins!

TAMAR AND JUDAH'S SONS

Judah had three sons, Er, Onan and Shelah. Now Judah took a wife for his firstborn son called Tamar and it seems that Er did not like his father's choice. Er was also wicked in the sight of the Lord (verse 7) and the Lord killed Him as punishment. Now Judah tells Onan (his second son), that he must marry Tamar and have a child in the name of his brother. This was a known Jewish custom at the time and Onan knew this, however, he was not interested in his father's faith. Instead, he agrees to marry Tamar and enjoys only the physical relationship with her by emitting outside of her. So God permitted that Onan die as punishment as well. Onan had no intention in fulfilling the law of God or the Jewish customs which he was raised up believing and thus, his punishment was just!

On the other hand, Tamar, who was not Jewish, was willing to follow the Jewish law. She did what Judah told her and kept herself a widow, waiting to be married to Judah's third son such that she might preserve the family lineage. The Gentile Tamar accepted the law

What the Fathers Say

By that one work of faith, Tamar became qualified to become a grandmother to Christ the Lord; to have her blood run in His veins. Matthew, the evangelist, included her name in the genealogy of the Lord Christ (Mat 1:223); whilst not including the names of Sarah, Rebecca and any of the other blessed mothers

– Fr. Tadros Malaty

of God but those born to a Jewish father did not! Now even though Judah told Tamar to wait for the third son in order to marry him, secretly he was worried for his third son in case he also dies if he marries Tamar. So he had no real intention of giving Tamar over to him. Thus, the wickedness of Judah was manifest in that even the Gentile woman Tamar was willing to accept the Jewish traditions, and Judah was not.

TAKING MATTERS INTO HER OWN HANDS

After a while, Judah's wife dies and eventually he goes away to celebrate and have a good time. Sheep shearing was known to be a time of festivity. Tamar finds out and realises that Judah is never really going to give her his third son Shelah as promised. Hence, she removes her widow's clothing and wraps herself, putting on a veil and waiting for Judah disguised as a harlot (prostitute). Now the Gentiles had an annual tradition where a lady would dress as a harlot and give herself to strangers, in return receiving a goat

The Other Tamar

People, Places &Things

In the Bible, there are two women named Tamar. Both of whom suffered because of forbidden sexual acts. We have talked about the first Tamar above, but who exactly is the second Tamar? Several centuries after the first Tamar, King David had a beautiful virgin daughter, who is also named Tamar. Because David had multiple wives, Tamar had several half-brothers. One brother, named Amnon, became infatuated and overcome with

lust towards Tamar because her beauty. With the help of cunning plot, Amnon pretend to be sick and got Tamar to nur him. When she came near t bed, he seized her and rap her. King David was outrage but surprisingly, did nothi to punish Amnon. Howev Absalom, one of Tamar's oth half-brothers, ordered servants to kill Amnon in an of rage and revenge.

as payment from the man, which she would then offer to her gods. Tamar tried following Judah's God and His laws but even Judah wouldn't follow them. Now, she is reverting to her own religious practices to make a point and ultimately preserve the lineage of Judah. Judah would have known that this is a pagan religious practice and that he had no right to take advantage of this for his own pleasure.

Now Tamar knew exactly what she wanted from Judah, his staff, cord and signet ring (verse 18) which Judah willingly gave her to assure her that he would return with the goat. However, Tamar did not even wait for Judah to bring back the goat. This was a one off action- she was fighting for her rights and fighting to preserve the lineage of Judah. After a few months, word got to Judah that Tamar was pregnant, and Judah infuriated, exclaims "let her be burned" (verse 24). Tamar shows Judah his staff, cord and signet ring, and immediately realises his unrighteousness, acknowledging that Tamar was more righteous than him for striving to keep God's laws.

Tamar has twins, Perez and Zerah, and from Perez's lineage comes David and eventually Christ. Now why would Christ come from such a sinful lineage? Why wouldn't he come from the lineage of someone righteous like Joseph instead? Again, this is a message of hope to all of us. With God, there is nothing impossible. He can turn sinners into saints. Therefore, we should never fall into the sin

What the Fathers Say

Yes, O Lord and King, grant me to see my own sin and not to judge my brother, for You are blessed from all ages to all ages. Amen

– St. Ephraim the Syrian

of despair, which is one of the devil's biggest traps preventing us from coming back to God. If we repent sincerely and confess our sins whole-heartedly, the Lord is willing to accept our repentance. Jesus came from the lineage of harlots and adulterers so that he could encourage that even the worst of the sinners is capable of change and repentance. Thus, Jesus Christ said: "Those who are well have no need of a physician, but those who are sick. I did not come to call the righteous, but sinners to repentance" (Mark 2: 17).

A STORY ON CONFESSION

St. Theophan the recluse tells the story of a youth who went to confession, ashamed and embarrassed at his many sins. Afterwards, he fell asleep and dreamt that he saw an angel who split open his chest with a knife, took out his heart, cut it into pieces and then removed the corrupt parts out of it. Then he carefully placed the heart back in its spot, and healed the wound as well. The youth woke up, overjoyed that his sins had been forgiven and his repentance and confession was accepted. Let us therefore comprehend and understand the power of repentance and confession, which has been administered to us for the forgiveness of sins and eternal life.

REFLECTION

When was the last time I sat with my father of confession? Do I take this sacrament seriously, and try and confess at least once every month?

CHAPTER 39

Events

CHAPTER 39

JOSEPH THE SUCCESSFUL MAN

In this chapter, Joseph begins to face even more trials and tribulations. Potiphar (who was Joseph's master) had a wife, who lusted over Joseph and desired to lie with him and commit sexual sin. Joseph is faced with a choice, either to succumb to the strong temptation and fall into sin, or to flee from sin and suffer the consequences, eventually being thrown into jail. Spiritually, the situation looks dire for Joseph, but the grace of God is still upon him. When we face tribulations in our lives, it does not mean that we have lost the grace of God. In fact, throughout our trials, the grace of God is usually greater!

Consider when Joseph was in his father' house, how he found favour in his father's eyes and lived an easy life. His brothers saw him as a dreamer and despised him. Also, there is no record that anything he touched was blessed or that he was a successful man. However, once he faces trials and hardships, the Bible tells us how successful Joseph has become and how God has blessed him (verses 2 and 3). Even Potiphar, who was a pagan (worshipper of idols) saw how blessed Joseph is and left all his household under his control and authority. It would have been so easy for Joseph to fall into sin and escape being thrown into jail, but Joseph preferred to follow the commandments of God above all.

There will be tribulations and hardships in the world but we have nothing to fear because Christ has overcome the world. This is a beautiful and comforting message that teaches us not to worry. The Lord Christ promised us "In the world you will have tribulations, but be of good cheer. I have overcome the world" (John 16:33). In another verse, Jesus pleads with us "Do not worry about tomorrow, for tomorrow will worry about itself. Sufficient for the day is its own troubles" (Mat 6: 34). If God loved us so much that he sent His only Son Jesus Christ to die for us, why would he ever deprive us of anything good? Therefore, rather than grumbling or complaining against God, we should always remember that we have a loving Father who only does what is best for His children!

JOSEPH VS POTIPHAR'S WIFE

When approached by Potiphar's wife, Joseph assessed the situation correctly and realised how wrong it would be for him to carry out this sin. Even though no one

What the Fathers Say

If you are still pure, be more so by avoiding looking at indecent things and hearing improper talks. Do not seek vain excuses, but only have one solution. Leave the Egyptian harlot and escape from her, even naked!

– St. John Chrysostom

Potiphar's Wife

The Bible does not give us much information about Potiphar's wife. We do not even know her name- the little that we do know comes from this small passage in the Bible. She resembles someone who is completely consumed by lustful pleasures and desires. She did not love Joseph, for if she did, she would not want to destroy him by sending him to jail. Neither did she love herself, for this sinful act would have brought great shame! She was not in love, but rather burning with the poison of lust which brings no real joy or comfort, only a temporary pleasure which leads to condemnation!

People, Places &Things

If you can follow Joseph's example, and leave your garment in the hand of your Egyptian mistress; in your nakedness you are following our Lord and Saviour who says in the Bible: 'whoever does not forsake all that he has to follow Me cannot be My disciple'

— St. Jerome

was watching them, Joseph knew that God Himself was watching and that this deed would displease the heart of God. Joseph questioned: "how then can I do this great wickedness, and sin against God?" (verse 9). We too, whenever we are tempted, should repeat Joseph's statement: "how then can I commit this sin against God?". This will help us to flee from temptations and overcome them. The fear and respect of God in our lives will give us strength, and even the mention of His name will cause the devil to flee in fear.

This story is the perfect motivation for us to flee from sexual sins. There is a frightening verse in Galatians 6:8- "he who sows to his flesh will of his flesh reap corruption". If I am involved in any sexual sins, whether this be pornography, an unhealthy relationship, adultery, fornication, or even just lustful glances, then I need to make an honest effort to stop immediately. Perhaps the greatest secret to Joseph's success was his purity! He persistently refused the joy of earthly pleasure, and therefore, God allowed him to be a participant in divine joy instead. There is a promise of success to all who are pure in heart. God reminds us of this in Job 22:30 "He will even deliver one who is not innocent; Yes, He will be delivered by the purity of your hands".

A SAINT'S ZEAL FOR PURITY

There are many stories of saints who went to extreme measures to protect their purity. After refusing to deny Christ, one saint was placed in a room with several prostitutes, so that they might fall into sin with him. After violently resisting, they bind him with chains such that the ladies might violate him and cause him to lose his purity. Restricted and unable to move, the Saint bit off his tongue and spit it at them! Immediately, the prostitutes fled in fear and repented of their wicked deeds, amazed at how much the Saint valued his purity. This Saint maintained his purity and the women became Christian! See how blessed the virtue of purity can be.

REFLECTION

Observe the great extent of Joseph's purity! He does not search after lust, but lust came chasing him, and even then, he chose the shame and humiliation of jail over displeasing God! Am I willing to take my search for purity this seriously?

Chapter 40

CHAPTER 40

Events

THE BUTLER AND THE BAKER

We have already talked about Joseph's dreams before, but now we realise that Joseph is also skilled at interpreting dreams as well! In this chapter, the butler and baker of Pharaoh are thrown into prison after offending Pharaoh. They both have dreams, and are distressed that no one can interpret them until they meet Joseph. Notice that Joseph even found favour in the eyes of the prison keeper, and was given freedom to deal with and serve the prisoners. The keeper has made Joseph second in charge of the prison (verse 4). This shows us how we find favour with people when God is walking with us and blessing our lives.

When Joseph finds the butler and baker upset, he inquires into the reason for their sadness. They disclose that each of them has had a dream, which they felt was a message about their fate with Pharaoh. In the Old Testament, dreams were often messages from God because He frequently spoke to His people through dreams and visions. Joseph interprets both dreams. The butler's dream was good and he would eventually be restored to his former position and serve Pharaoh again. Meanwhile, the baker's dream was bad; he would be killed by Pharaoh in three days.

SPEAKING THE TRUTH

In all this, Joseph is both genuine and honest in delivering the word of God. He doesn't try gloss over the bad news to the baker but instead, he is straight forward and tells both men exactly what is to happen to them. This is another extremely important practical message for us in our lives today. Unfortunately, in today's society, we do not like to think of the consequences of our actions and our sins.

When famous Australian rugby union player Israel Folau was asked by a supporter about the consequences of living a homosexual life, he replied "hell, unless the person repents of their sins". We know that this is the truth because 1 Cor 6:9 states that "neither fornicators, nor adulterers, nor homosexuals, nor thieves" will enter the kingdom of heaven (unless they repent of their sins, then God is more than happy to accept their repentance of course!). Folau faced a huge backlash from the media, receiving hate messages, insults and eventually, his multi-million dollar rugby union contract was torn up! His response? "I would sooner lose everything, friends, family, possessions, my football career, the lot, and still stand with Jesus, than have all of those things and not stand beside Him".

> **What the Fathers Say**
>
> Joseph, eager to be released from prison, was left there for some time so as to learn to not put his hope or trust in humans, but in God alone
>
> – St. John Chrysostom

The Butler and the Baker: the Two Thieves on The Cross

The butler and baker probably refer to the two robbers, who were crucified with the Lord Christ- the true Joseph, and were blaspheming Him. But the one on the right proclaimed his repentance and took hold of paradise to remain with God. Meanwhile, the one on the left, remained in his evil and blasphemed, losing both his present and eternal life. The two officers refer to the fallen mankind, yet some of them crossed over wrath to Paradise, whilst others, in their denial, eternally lost their lives.

People, Places &Things

Joseph lived in his prison as if he were in his own house, caring for other prisoners as if they were part of his own family. He was characterised by meekness, tenderness and obedience; He was not ashamed of his servitude, nor his prison, but was compassionate to all, serving all, even the fiercest of prisoners. So Joseph was prosperous wherever he went

— St. John Chrysostom

We too should have courage to speak the truth in a loving manner. If we see our friend walking into a hole and have the chance to save them, wouldn't we at least warn them there's a hole, even if that isn't exactly what they want to hear? We should never shy away from speaking the truth, regardless of what people may say or think of us. St. Paul himself said this when He exclaimed: "The message of the cross is foolishness to those who are perishing, but to us who are being saved it is the power of God" (1 Cor 1: 18).

JOSEPH THE FORGIVING

In this chapter, Joseph also shows that he is an honorable man. He tells the butler that he was stolen from home and has done nothing wrong in Egypt to deserve imprisonment. He makes no accusations against his brothers or Potiphar and his wife. Joseph is not interested in blaming anyone, he only wants to be freed because he has been falsely accused. He doesn't present himself as a victim and does not speak ill of anyone. This incident shows us Joseph's forgiving nature. He does not bear a grudge against those who have hurt him, instead choosing to forgive them. We too must forgive all those who have wronged us. After all, we ask God every single day to "Forgive us our trespasses, as we forgive those who trespass against us". Therefore, we cannot expect God to forgive our sins, unless we too have forgiven those who have wronged us!

REFLECTION

In a world which often opposes the commandments and teachings of God, am I also ashamed of the gospel of Christ? Or am I willing to preach and publicly proclaim my faith, even at the expense of how other people perceive me?

CHAPTER 41

GENESIS FOR TEENS

DREAMS, DREAMS AND MORE DREAMS

Two years have passed since Joseph interpreted the dreams of the baker and butler. Now Pharaoh also has two dreams that no one could interpret, neither the magicians, nor the wise man. They are the same dreams, just repeated in different forms. The fathers believe that Pharaoh's dreams are a message from God, and since any dream of God cannot be interpreted by the devil, therefore none of the magicians could interpret the dream.

In Pharaoh's first dream, seven thin and bony cows ate up the seven fat and beautiful cows. In the second dream, seven thin, dry heads of grain began to swallow up the seven good, ripe heads of grain. Joseph's interpretation is simple: there will be seven years of plentiful harvest in the land, followed by seven years of severe bareness and famine. Not only does Joseph interpret the meaning of the dream, but he also gives a wise suggestion to Pharaoh about how to deal with the famine that was about to come. Joseph could have simply stopped speaking after he interpreted the dreams, but was guided by the Holy Spirit to advise Pharaoh about how to approach the situation.

On a quick side note, Joseph is now going to become second in charge of Egypt behind Pharaoh. This is a huge position of power, and Joseph had to wait a long time to get there. But during this time, he never lost faith or hope in God. He never blamed God and remained

Events

CHAPTER 41

with God throughout his tribulations. In the same way, God often makes us wait when we ask for something. When we are in any tribulation or trial, this is usually the time when we are closest to God. Our prayers increase, our Bible readings increase and our repentance and confession becomes more regular. This is because we are waiting on the Lord. However, if everything is smooth in our life, we may become spiritually carless and lukewarm. God doesn't want us to experience hardships, but He cares for our eternity above all. So when we face trials and tribulations, we should use this as an opportunity to get closer to God. Pope Shenouda even used to pray: "God those things which bring me closer to You, bring them closer to me and those things which take me away from You, take them away from me".

JOSEPH BECOMES SECOND IN CHARGE

Throughout this incident, Pharaoh observes Joseph's great wisdom and recognises that he is a great man who is

What the Fathers Say

How much do we need to set forth from the magicians and wise men to the True Joseph, not to lean any more on human understanding ; but with faith encountering the Lord Jesus Christ, to reveal to us the divine mysteries to the perfection of His eternal glory – Fr. Tadros Malaty

Pharaoh's Signet Ring

Pharaoh is amazed by the wisdom and genuineness of Joseph, and questions: "Can we find such a one as this, a man in whom is the spirit of God?". Pharaoh then makes Joseph ruler over all his house, and places him second on the throne (only under Pharaoh). As a testimony of this, Pharaoh removes the signet ring from his hand and places it on Joseph's hand. This act in itself is symbolic of marriage. the husband places the ring on the hand of his wife, and he entrusts her with the responsibility of his entire household. In a similar manner, through this act, Pharaoh displays his complete and absolute trust in Joseph to rule over the land of Egypt.

People, Places &Things

GENESIS FOR TEENS

What the Fathers Say

This is the way we should see Christ. He is our friend, our brother; He is whatever is good and beautiful. He is everything. Yet, He is still a friend and He shouts it out, "You're my friends, don't you understand that? We're brothers. I don't hold hell in my hands. I am not threatening you. I love you. I want you to enjoy life together with me

– Elder Porphyrios

guided by God. It was as if Pharaoh recognised the spirit of God inside of Joseph. God always reveals Himself and shows his glory when needed. This is seen throughout various situations in the Old Testament. For example, when the three youth were thrown into the fire, the Gentiles saw 4 and not 3 people. God was with the youth and revealed Himself to the unbelievers (Daniel 3:25). God can use us too to give messages to non-believers! We are his candles in a dark world, and just have to trust Him like Joseph did. In this situation, God will show His power and glory to everyone.

Look at the amazing transformation that took place over the last few chapters. In chapter 37, Joseph was thrown by his brothers into the pit and sold as a slave. Then in chapter 39, Joseph was thrown into jail for refusing to fall into sin. And now in chapter 41, Joseph has become second in charge of Egypt! Joseph never grumbled against God, and genuinely trusted in God's will. It would have been so easy for Joseph to doubt God whilst he was in the pit, sold as a slave or behind bars in prisons. But he always trusted God and never worried! We too as Christians should never worry, even if our earthly lives are filled with problems. Instead we ought to pray: "Your will be done O God", and have faith that God cares about us even more than we care about ourselves, and that His will is the best possible outcome for our lives.

REFLECTION

Is there a trial or tribulation from which I am suffering? Have I looked in my heart, and searched it? Maybe there is a particular sin which I am repeating? Maybe God is using this trial or tribulation to lead me on the path of repentance?

CHAPTER 42

Events

CHAPTER 42

He knows us, but we don't know Him

In this chapter, Jacob and his family begin to suffer from starvation due to the famine. Jacob knows that there is food in Egypt, and realises that the only solution is to send his sons to go and collect some supplies. In verses 6-8, the brothers came to Egypt and meet Joseph. He immediately recognised them but they did not know him. The analogy is that they came looking for the Messiah. He knew them, but they did not know Him. The same applies to Christ. We may not recognise Him and His work in our lives, but He always knows us. Even in our most sinful states when we are so far away from God, He still values and treasures us as His children. Therefore, regardless of how far we have strayed from Him, he still knows us, loves us and is waiting for us to return.

God's love is unconditional, He loved us before we were even made, and His love does not change depending on any circumstances! Even if we live a life which is so full of fear, guilt, anxiety, despair or total sin, rest assured, God has never left us! This is what David says in the psalms: "Where can I go from Your spirit? Or where can I flee from Your presence? If I ascend into heaven, You are there; if I make my bed in hell, behold, You are there" (Ps 139: 7-8).

St. Moses the Strong

This is evident in the life of St. Moses the Strong (also known as Moses the black). He was a man so immersed in sin. He was a gang leader, thief, adulterer and even a murderer! There was no sin he didn't commit! However, one day he looked up to heaven and asked: "O God whom I do not know, let me know you". He heard a voice from heaven instructing him to travel to Wadi El-Natroun (a monastery in Egypt), where St. Isidorous explained to him everything about Christianity. He was baptised, ordained as a monk and then became the leader of 4000 monks! Eventually, he was even martyred for the sake of Christ. When the Barbarians came to attack the monastery, he had the opportunity to flee with the other monks. Instead, he chose to die, exclaiming that "those who live by the sword will die by the sword" (Mat 26:52). This is a message of great hope, no matter how bad we may think we are going in our spiritual lives! Have you lost hope in your spiritual life? Remember that God "is able to raise up to Abraham children from these stones?" (Mat 3:9), and you are far more valuable than many stones!

What the Fathers Say

When you behold a certain trial or tribulation that happened to you, remember your sins which brought this upon you

– St. John Chrysostom

Jacob or Israel?

In verse 1, Joseph's father is referred to as Jacob and not Israel. When the Bible uses "Jacob", it is alluding to the Jews, who lost faith in Christ the Lord, namely, the true Joseph. Meanwhile, when the name "Israel" is used in the Bible, it refers to the chosen people of God. Therefore, when the Jews were obedient to God, they are the "children of Israel", and when they disobey God, they are referred to as the "children of Jacob". Similarly, we cannot truly maintain our identity as children of God unless we whole-heartedly believe in Him and follow His commands.

People, Places &Things

What the Fathers Say

God, in His love, sometimes seems rough, not to deprive us of His compassion, but to realise His plans in us, and to enter with us into His mysteries, and to let us enjoy His grace, in an exalted way, which is beyond our human comprehension

— Fr. Tadros Malaty

FAMILY REUNION

In verses 21-23, the brothers confess what they did to Joseph and express their guilt. They begin to realise that the trials they are going though in life are as a result of what they did to Joseph. Finally their consciences are being awakened! Sometimes, we also push God to put us in the same situation. We force Him to give us trials so we can confess our sins and repent of our evil deeds. God's ultimate goal is our salvation, not our happiness on earth (although God does not ever want us to be miserable!). Therefore, we should always look at trials in our life through the same lens as God. Maybe these events are helping me come closer to God and granting me salvation.

Then in verse 24, Joseph turns away from his brothers and weeps. This shows us that Joseph's ultimate intention is not to hurt his brothers, but rather bring them to salvation. He is waiting for them and wants to reveal himself to them, but only when he is sure that they have repented from their crooked ways. In Job 5: 17, it is written: "'Behold, happy is the man whom God corrects; Therefore do not despise the chastening of the Almighty. For He bruises, but He binds up; He wounds, but His hands make whole." God wants our salvation first and foremost, and there are many people now in Hades who desire one more moment on earth to repent. For them, it is now too late. But for us, let us use the opportunities we have to repent and return to God whilst we still have the chance! Let us learn from the trial or tribulation in our life and wake up from our sinful state while we have the opportunity to do so!

Eventually, Joseph provides them food and sends them on their way home, but holds Simeon as a hostage until they return again to Egypt with Benjamin. Joseph also does something extremely amazing and returns each man's money to them, even giving them provisions for the journey (verse 25). When they eventually return home (without Simeon), they recount to Jacob all that happened in Egypt and inform him that Benjamin is required to travel to Egypt as well. Whilst he is initially reluctant, Jacob eventually realises that he has no choice but to oblige.

REFLECTION

Do thoughts of despair or hopelessness ever consume me and fill my heart? Let us learn to remember that God's love for me is unconditional, and does not rely on my own goodness!

CHAPTER 43

JACOB'S DILEMMA

Jacob faces a huge dilemma. The food has once again run out, and Jacob tells his sons to go buy some more from Egypt. Whilst this seems like a simple task, Jacob's sons know very well that they will not receive food from Joseph unless Benjamin goes with them. If Jacob refuses, they won't go and will eventually starve to death. Jacob has already lost two sons, Joseph and Simeon, and could not bear to lose Benjamin as well!

In verses 1-5, notice again that the father is referred to as Jacob because he is weak and not accepting. However, in verse 6 he is referred to as Israel because he is about to have a change of heart. He is about to give in to Joseph's demands and accept what has to be done. Just like in the last chapter, when we do God's will we are Israel, we are God's children. Meanwhile when we follow our own will, we are Jacob and not the children of God.

Jacob tells them to take Benjamin and prays that Joseph will have mercy on them, return Benjamin and release Simeon. In verse 14, Jacob cries: "If I am bereaved, I am bereaved". The fathers tell us that he is surrendering to God- essentially, Jacob is finally submitting to God's will. As good Christians, we should learn to do the same and leave everything in the hand of God. He is our creator and cares for us even more than ourselves. Therefore in our prayers, instead of asking God for so many earthly requests

Events

CHAPTER 43

and desires, it is sufficient for us to pray that God's will be done, and trust that His will is always the best outcome for us. Remember the many promises of God: "the very hairs of your head are all numbered" (Luke 12:7), "I have inscribed you on the palms of My hands" (Isaiah 49:16) and "When my father and mother forsake me, the Lord will take care of me" (Psalm 27: 10). Thus, for those who believe in the love and mercy of God, it seems only logical to have complete confidence and faith in Him.

WHAT HAPPENED WITH THE MONEY?

In verses 15-17, the brothers take Benjamin and double the money to Egypt to stand before Joseph. Initially, the brothers are afraid to return to Joseph because they suspect that they might be accused of stealing the money that was placed in their money sacks. They defend themselves, and Joseph's steward reassures them that everything will be alright. It appears that Joseph didn't asked the steward to return their money, instead he paid them out with his own money. As a representative of Christ, the fathers tell us that Christ is the one who must pay the price

> **What the Fathers Say**
>
> Let us be like Joseph, to be sad and to weep for those who harm us. Let us not get angry with them, as they actually are worthy of tears, because of the punishment that awaits them, and the judgement which they cast upon themselves
>
> – St. John Chrysostom

Joseph's Chamber

When Joseph sets his eyes on his younger brother Benjamin, he cannot contain his emotions, and thus goes into his chamber and weeps, washing his face and restraining himself saying: "Serve the bread". What is that "chamber" where the true Joseph wept, then washed His face, and came out, but His Holy tomb, where He encountered death. Christ washed our death, not by His tears, but by His pure blood. Further, Christ resurrected to give us His risen body, so that we might be able to enjoy eternal life with Him!

People, Places &Things

What the Fathers Say

We suffer because we have no humility and because we do not love our brother. From the love of our brother comes the love of God. People do not learn humility and because of their pride, they cannot receive the grace of the Holy Spirit. Therefore, the whole world suffers

— Silouan the Athonite

of our sins. We can have as many virtues as we like, but it is Christ who paid the ransom that allowed us back into heaven. God is the one who saves us, it is not our goodness, but His love. Without the sacrifice of Jesus Christ's blood on the Cross, there is no salvation and no eternal life.

JOSEPH'S DREAMS COME TRUE

Remember in chapter 37, when Joseph dreamt that all his brothers would bow down to him? He did not dream this once, but rather twice! And now in this chapter, the brothers bow down to Joseph twice. Once in verse 26 and again in verse 28! This is a fulfilment of the prophesies, proving the validity of Joseph's dreams and reaffirming that he is truly a man of God who was divinely inspired.

Now Joseph instructs his men to prepare a feast for his brothers, and orders that Benjamin's serving be five times the size of his brother's servings. Now why exactly is this the case, especially given that Benjamin is the youngest son? The father's believe that Joseph was testing his brothers to see if they would be jealous- but there was no reaction from them, and this assured Joseph that they were cured of their jealous ways. Some of the fathers also believe that Benjamin is given more than his brothers because: "The first will be last and the last will be first" (Mat 20: 16) which encourages us to pursue a life of humility.

ST. MACARIUS THE GREAT: AN EXAMPLE OF HUMILITY

There are many examples of humility in our modern church. None more than the St. Macarius the great. When he lived in the desert alone in solitude, a woman accused him of seducing her and eventually impregnating her in order to cover up for her sinful act of fornication. The people of the community dragged St. Macarius in the streets and hurled insults at him. He endured the tribulation with great humility, and even sent the money he got from weaving baskets to support this pregnant woman. The innocence of Saint Macarius was manifested when the woman, who suffered torment for many days, was not able to give birth. She confessed that she had slandered the hermit, and revealed the name of the real father. When her parents found out the truth, they were astonished and intended to go to the saint to ask forgiveness. Though Saint Macarius willingly accepted dishonour, he escaped from the praise of man and fled the village before anyone could apologise to him.

REFLECTION

Do I become jealous or envious when my brother or sister is successful or finds favour instead of me? Let us learn from the example of Joseph's brothers, who were once consumed with pride, but eventually acquired the virtue of humility.

CHAPTER 44

PLOT TWIST

In the previous chapter, Joseph arranged a banquet for his brothers. Now in verses 1-13 of this chapter, we see a twist in events. Joseph has a plan, which he begins to execute. He secretly has his own silver cup which he places into Benjamin's sack as the brothers are about to leave and go back home. Joseph still has some doubts about his brothers. He tested their loyalty towards Simeon and they passed the test and returned to him with Benjamin as requested. Now Joseph is about to test their loyalty again and see how they will react when Benjamin is in trouble. He is still unsure if they will treat Benjamin the same way that they treated him and wants to see if they save themselves and flee, leaving Benjamin to become a slave.

If their brothers had abandoned Benjamin, then Joseph would have exposed them for their treatment of Benjamin as well as their treatment of him all those years ago. If his brothers defend Benjamin, then they would have passed the test and found favour in Joseph's eyes. In either situation, Joseph would have been victorious because he would have his beloved Benjamin and would have called his father to come too. Therefore, putting the cup in Benjamin's bag was a very wise decision!

LEARNING FROM THEIR MISTAKES

Notice that the brothers behave extremely admirably. It would have been so

Events

CHAPTER 44

easy for them to leave Benjamin as a slave and return home, but they adamantly refused to do so. In verse 13, they even tore their clothes out of sadness and guilt- they are repenting and blaming themselves for what was happening to Benjamin. In verses 14-17, Joseph again wants to test his brother's sincerity. Judah is the one who speaks out because he is the one who made the oath with his father that Benjamin would return home safely. Then, Judah publicly confesses his guilt! Which guilt is this since they didn't steal the cup? Judah is publicly confessing of selling Joseph all those years ago, and admitting that he is wrong. Joseph was testing his brothers, and it appears that they have learnt from their previous mistakes.

Judah's speech is very humble, respectful and void of aggression. He outlines the entire story with no hard feelings. Judah mentions

What the Fathers Say

It is madness for a Christian to be envious. In Christ, we have all received infinitely great blessings

– St John of Kronstadt

Joseph's Cup

Joseph cunningly hides his silver cup in Benjamin's sack, and after sending his brothers on their way home, instructs his men to chase after the brothers. Joseph has a specific plan, and wants to put his brother's loyalty to the test. Now what is this cup, found in the sack of Benjamin, that made all of them return to Joseph, but the cup that the Lord Christ drank our sake when He said: "O My Father, if it is possible, let this cup pass from Me. Nevertheless, not as I will but as You will" (Mat 26: 39). The Lord drank this cup on behalf of all humanity, and by drinking it, He restored us back to the Holy City. Joseph's steward said: "With whoever of your servants it (the cup) is found, let him die" (verse 9). This is the exact same voice of humanity which cried out: "It was expedient that one man should die for the people" (John 18:14). The Lord Christ bore the cup for our sake, and likewise He willingly took the punishment of death on our behalf.

People, Places &Things

What the Fathers Say

In the end of times, a man will be saved by love, humbleness and kindness. Kindness will open the gates of heaven; humbleness will lead him into Heaven and love will allow him to see God

— St. Gregory of Georgia

that Jacob had two sons from one wife and that he loves them dearly- Judah does so with no anger or envy. This is very different to the envy he previously had in his heart towards Joseph. At this stage, Joseph's heart is being moved as Judah mentions his concern for his father's health and wellbeing. Previously, when they sold Joseph, they did not care about the effects upon their father because they were so engulfed in jealousy and envy. Now that these feelings are gone and they have repented, the brothers can empathise with their father and care for his feelings.

See how much envy and jealousy blind us to how much harm we are causing others! Envy and jealousy can cause us to have hate towards others, even to the extent of wishing bad things upon them- some even to the point of killing! Recall that Cain killed Abel out of envy (Genesis 4). Pilate knew that the Jews also wanted to kill Jesus out of envy. Now that we see how Judah is free of envy and jealousy, he is even willing to sacrifice himself in the place of Benjamin (verse 33)! He is not only trying to free Benjamin, but willing to even accept the punishment on his behalf! Judah was determined to keep the promise he made to his father, and this is the result of repentance. When we repent, hate and envy becomes transformed into love and sacrifice!

LOVE AND NOT HATE

Notice how much Joseph's brothers are transformed in this chapter. The same people that sold their brother out of jealousy were willing to sacrifice their lives for the sake of their brother in this chapter. This is a sign of true love which is the mother of all virtues. When the Lord Christ was asked about which commandments are the greatest, his answer was clear: love God and love your neighbour (Mark 12: 28-31). This is sufficient for us to enter the kingdom of heaven. So let us make it an absolute priority in our lives to love God, and to love our brethren unconditionally because at the end of the day, love will cover a multitude of sins. (1 Peter 4:8)

REFLECTION

Am I willing to learn from my mistakes, and use them to grow and mature spiritually? The brothers of Joseph did, and made sure that they did not fall into the same mistake twice!

CHAPTER 45

Events

CHAPTER 45

JOSEPH CAN'T CONTROL HIS EMOTIONS

In this chapter, Joseph can no longer control his emotions and cries out "Make everyone go out from me!" before making himself known to his brothers. This great emotion shows that Joseph did not cruelly manipulate his brothers, but was directed by God to test them. The brothers were "dismayed in his presence", and are terrified regarding the possible consequences of their actions- they believe that Joseph may seek revenge for all that has happened. But instead, Joseph exclaims: "God sent me before you to preserve you and save your lives" (verse 7).

Notice how Joseph sees God's hands in every single situation! All of Joseph's sorrows were for a purpose. God used them to preserve his family, allowing it to grow and become a great nation and a distinctive people. This shows the heart of those who trust in God. They are not vindictive or vengeful when things go wrong, but instead forgive and cover the sins of their brethren. It would not have been easy for Joseph to forgive his brothers after causing him so much harm, Not only did they sell him as a slave and throw him into a pit, they even sent him to exile and jail. But Joseph does not remember this, and has only love in his heart for his brothers.

FORGIVE AND YOU WILL BE FORGIVEN

When Jesus was asked by his disciples how to pray, he recited the famous "Our Father" prayer, and after he finished, he made only one small comment on the prayer: "If you do not forgive others their sins, your Father will not forgive your sins". This was the only segment of the "Our Father" prayer which our Lord found it necessary to comment on. The equation is simple; all men are sinners, and we cannot ask God to forgive us our sins, if we do not forgive those who have wronged us.

There is a famous story of two men who hated each other, and could not see eye to eye. They went to many counsellors, priests and church servants, to find a way to reconcile and set aside their differences. Nothing worked. They then went to St. Abraam Bishop of Fayoum, who listened to their arguments for a whole hour, without opening his mouth. When they finished arguing, without saying a word, St. Abraam stood up to pray the "Our Father", and instead of saying "Forgive us our trespasses as we forgive those who trespass

What the Fathers Say

We all have to die, beloved brethren. And it will be hard for us, if, while we are in this world, we do not love each other, if we are not reconciled with our enemies, and if we do not forgive the one who has grieved us

– Pope Shenouda III

Joseph's three encounters with his brethren

Joseph's first encounter with his brothers took place in the presence of many, as did the second encounter. But in the third encounter, Joseph did not reveal himself until he drove all the strangers outside, exclaiming: "Make everyone go out from me" (verse 1). Similarly, the first encounter with Christ at the Cross occurred before a multitude of people, and likewise the second encounter of his burial occurred before the Roman guards. But on His resurrection, He did not reveal Himself except to His own, who yearn for the resurrected life. In other words, the crucifixion and burial were realised in public, to proclaim His salvation to all mankind. As for the resurrection, it was not to be enjoyed except by those who wish to recognise its mysteries, and enjoy His risen life!

People, Places &Things

In amazing tenderness, and in order to root out their fear, Joseph says to them: "please come near me" (verse 4). Through sin, we distance ourselves from our Joseph, yet, as we Hear his voice and receive the work of His resurrection in us, we "come near Him" and as the apostle Paul said: "But now in Christ Jesus, you who once were far off, have been made near by the blood of Christ" (Ephesians 2: 13)

- Fr. Tadros Malaty

against us", he said "Do not forgive us our trespasses, as we do not forgive those who trespass against us". Immediately, both men were filled with remorse and regret, embraced each other, and agreed to reconcile with one another.

JOSEPH IS ALIVE

After this emotional encounter, Joseph sends his brothers back to Israel to proclaim the good news to his father Jacob; that Joseph is alive and not dead! However, in verse 26, we learn that Jacob "did not believe them". When Jacob was informed that Joseph was dead many chapters ago, he believed straight away! Now, when he is informed that Joseph is in fact alive, Jacob doubts. In a similar manner, the only way people will know that Jesus is alive is if we tell them, and show them His blessings in our lives. If we call ourselves Christians and swear, gossip, judge and hate our fellow brethren, we make a mockery of our Christianity and our faith will appear to be in vain.

Mother Teresa once famously quoted "You may be the only Bible that people read". We should always remember that we are living representatives of Christ on earth. Therefore, we are called to be different. Most people in this world hold grudges, but we are called to love those who hate us and bless those who curse us. Most people in this world fall into sexual sins daily, but we are called to be pure in order to see God. Most people in this world become anxious and depressed when facing trials and tribulations, but we are called to trust God unconditionally and believe whole-heartedly in Him.

REFLECTION

Do I have the same spirit of love which Joseph did? Instead of seeking revenge upon those who wronged me, do I have a spirit of peace and love towards them?

CHAPTER 46

GENESIS FOR TEENS

GOD SPEAKS TO JACOB

Events

CHAPTER 46

In this chapter, God appears to Jacob, comforting and reassuring him that everything will be ok. Realise that more than 40 years before, when Jacob was about to leave the Promised Land, God spoke to him in a dream. Now, when he is about to leave the land again, God again reassures him through a dream. God tells Jacob: "Do not fear to go down to Egypt"- indicating that Jacob was scared and reluctant to go to Egypt. Jacob may have remembered when Abraham went down to Egypt previously in the time of famine (Genesis 12: 10-20) and how much hardship this caused. He may also have remembered how God told his father Isaac not to go down to Egypt (Genesis 26:2). Ultimately, God wants to comfort and reassure Jacob that everything is going to end up just fine!

If God was to appear to us today, most likely he would have a similar message for us. In today's world, everyone is filled with stress, anxiety and worry. Maybe it could be an exam, an illness, or a family problem. The bottom line is, everyone in this world has something to stress and be anxious about. But today God has a message for us too: "Do not fear", a message which was repeated 365 times in the Bible, one time for every day. When a famous sportsman was asked how he had the nerve to perform in front of hundreds of thousands of supporters every single week, he replied: "I know that even if I bottle it all and stuff up completely, I know that I'll go home and my mum will still love me". It's the same with us. Even if our lives are filled with stresses, troubles, mistakes and worries, we can rest assured that we can go home and God will still love us too! We can be 100% sure that God did not create us to live in fear, "For God has not given us a spirit of fear, but of power and of love and of a sound mind" (2 Tim 1: 7).

DO NOT WORRY

The Bible is filled with promises. It's as if God is begging us not to worry! In Isaiah 49:15, God asks: "Can a woman forget her nursing child... Surely, they may forget, Yet I will not forget you". Can a mother forget her newborn baby? Impossible. But God is telling us, that EVEN if she does forget (which will really never happen), He will still not forget us. Then in the following verse, another beautiful promise. God says in Isaiah 49: 16- "Behold, I have inscribed you on the palms of My hand". That's right- in the palm of His hand! It's as

What the Fathers Say

I realised that we all worry about ourselves too much and that only he who leaves everything to the will of God can feel truly joyous, light and peaceful

- Elder Thaddeus of Vitovnica

Why does God choose Judah?

Judah leads the way for his brothers in their journey to Egypt, and Judah is also the one who is chosen to bear the Messiah. From the lineage of Judah comes the Lord Jesus Christ, many generations later. Now why is this the case? Wasn't Judah's household full of problems and sin (refer to chapter 38)? Not only this, but David (who came from the lineage of Judah) was also a murderer and adulterer, and from this same lineage came Rahab the harlot? Perhaps this is to teach us that Jesus came from the sinners, and His love for us does not depend on our sins or weaknesses. Also, when Benjamin was going to be taken away by Joseph as captive in Chapter 44, Judah pleads: "let your servant remain instead of the lad as a slave to my lord" (Gen 44:33). This sacrificial act is symbolic of the Lord Christ, who took the punishment of death on our behalf.

People, Places &Things

if God has a tattoo of us on the palm of His hand (not an actual tattoo of course!), but essentially, God is trying to say that we are a part of Him and He will never ever forget us!

A study conducted by leading psychologists and scientists in the USA found that amongst 500 people, there existed 7,000 unique fears- averaging to 14 individual fears per person. This highlights the great extent of anxiety and worry which we live within today's society. We have become captives, almost enslaved to our fears, and perhaps this has prevented us from enjoying the divine love of God in our lives. God has a perfect plan for each and every one of us. Not just for today or tomorrow, but the rest of our lives. This is a divine promise which was given from the mouth of God in Jeremiah 29:11 "For I know the thoughts that I think toward you, says the Lord, thoughts of peace and not evil, to give you a future and a hope".

JUDAH LEADS THE WAY

The rest of this chapter is quite uneventful, as Jacob and his children make their way to Egypt. Notice that Judah leads the way in verse 28. The fathers contemplate and say that, since from Judah comes the Saviour Jesus Christ, it is only fitting that Judah leads his brothers to Egypt. Christ is the only one who can satisfy our hunger and thirst, in the same way that Judah leads his brothers to Egypt to end their physical hunger. Remember what the Lord says in Mat 11:28 "Come to Me,

What the Fathers Say

If you are in great troubles, fear, pain and sadness, and the enemy has been stalking you day and night, you shouldn't be afraid or scared, as it is not the end. The happy end is coming, and the Lord will come. He is sleeping just because you are sleeping, awake Him to rebuke the wind

– Fr. Matthew the Poor

all you are weary and carry heavy burdens and I will give you rest".

Notice that in the last verse of the chapter, Joseph also prepares a place for his brothers and father to dwell in Goshen. God had a place for His people. He didn't bring them to Egypt just to provide them with food alone, which is what they came for, but he provided them with a new home. In a similar manner, Jesus takes care of us in the present, but also in the future and in the kingdom of heaven as well- where he has already prepared a place for us!

REFLECTION

Why do I always worry? Why is my life filled with fear and anxiety? I should learn to throw everything at the feet of God, and trust in His infinite love for me!

CHAPTER 47

Events

CHAPTER 47

JOSEPH'S BROTHERS RECEIVE BLESSING

When Jacob and his sons finally arrive in Egypt, they meet Pharaoh in order to decide their fate. Even though Joseph had extremely high status in the government of Egypt, the family still had to ask permission to dwell in the land of Goshen. Pharaoh agrees that Joseph's brothers and their father should "dwell in the best of the land" (verse 6). This blessing was all because of Joseph. He saved Egypt and much of the world from famine, and now the whole family of Jacob was blessed as a result.

Notice that since Joseph became a blessing, his whole family too was blessed! This is the effect that we can have on our family and friends if even one righteous person exists within our family/friendship group/community, God can show mercy on everyone as a result. As said by St Seraphim of Sarov, "Acquire a peaceful spirit [with Christ], and thousands around you will be saved."

When the famous monk Abouna Abdel-Mesih el Habashi (the Ethiopian) desired to live an ascetic life in the desert and leave his cell in the monastery, the abbot of the monastery refused adamantly. So Abouna Abdel-Mesih disobeyed, and escaped the monastery to live in the desert anyways. The abbot was furious at Abouna's disobedience and complained to Pope Kyrillos the 6th, the patriarch at the time. Much to the abbot's surprise, Pope Kyrillos replied: "Leave Abouna Abdel-Mesih to do whatever he pleases, for

God's wrath is lifted from the earth as a result of his prayers". See the effect that just one righteous person can have!

JACOB BLESSES PHARAOH

When Pharaoh meets Jacob, he asks him, "How old are you?" and Jacob replies "The days of the years of my pilgrimage are one hundred and thirty years" (verse 9). See how beautiful this response is! Instead of simply replying "130 years", he says "the days of my pilgrimage are one hundred and thirty years". Jacob explains that he is on a pilgrimage and knows that his real home is somewhere else, in heaven. In the liturgy, the priest also prays "And we too who are pilgrims in this world, keep us in your faith". It is always important for us to remember that we are not made for this world, but for another. Therefore, if we are overly attached to anything in this world,

> **What the Fathers Say**
>
> You must not be greatly troubled about many things, but you should care for the main thing, preparing yourself for death
>
> - St. Ambrose

Jacob's Dying Wish

After 130 years on earth, Jacob recognises that his days are numbered and has one final request to Joseph; "Do not bury me in Egypt, but let me lie with my fathers; you shall carry me out of Egypt and bury me in their burial place". Jacob wishes to be buried in Canaan, the "Promised Land", rather than in Egypt. But why is Jacob so adamant on this? One reason for this has to do with God's promise that Abraham's descendants would possess the land where he had been buried (Gen 12: 1-3). Jacob knew that if he was buried in Canaan, his tomb would forever remain in the Promised Land. Another reason for this is because Jacob wanted to be buried with his family, as a sign of love and solidarity. Abraham too was buried there, as was his son Isaac and also Jacob's wife as well. Finally, Jacob preferred to be buried in the land which he and his family owned, rather than being buried in the land of foreigners in Egypt.

> **People, Places &Things**

we must distance ourselves from it and remember that only God really matters. Even if we live one-hundred years on earth, death is still a reality and thus we must remember that our homes are elsewhere.

After this, Jacob reflects: "few and evil have been the days of the years of my life". This was not a cynical statement by Jacob, but a reflective one where he recollects all his short-comings and mistakes. Again, Jacob is looking forward to a better life ahead, the eternal life. A wise man once said that no one goes to war to enjoy the war, but to enjoy the victory that comes afterwards. We too should apply this to our lives, we can still enjoy it of course! But this joy should come from being with Christ and not from any external riches or pleasures. Our life on earth is merely a preparation for the eternal joy which comes from a life with God in heaven.

JOSEPH'S VOW TO JACOB

Joseph displays his excellent administrative skills as well, bargaining with the people of the land and providing them with food in return for their goods and their services. Then in verses 28-31, a very poignant and touching moment takes place. Jacob recognises that his days are numbered, and he asks his son Joseph to bury him with his fathers and not in Egypt! Jacob knew that Egypt was not his home, and that he belonged in the land promised to his descendants. He recognised and understood that he was

What the Fathers Say

Be of good courage, all you dead, for death is slain and hell despoiled; the crucified and risen Christ is King. He has given incorruption to our flesh; he raises us and grants us resurrection and counts us worthy of his joy and glory

– St. Isaac the Syrian

the inheritor of Abraham's covenant. Jacob then bows himself on the head of the bed, recognising that his days are almost coming to an end.

REFLECTION

No matter how many years we live on earth, all of us will die and then rise again in the second coming. Do I spend my time on earth productively, remembering that my faith and works on earth, will determine how I spend my eternity?

CHAPTER 48

Events

CHAPTER 48

REMEMBERING GOD'S PROMISES

In this chapter, Jacob is ageing and senses that his death is near. So Jacob calls for Joseph to bless his two sons, Ephraim and Manasseh. Jacob reminds Joseph of God's promise to their father Abraham: "Behold, I will make you fruitful and multiply you, and I will make of you a multitude of people" (Genesis 17: 2, 6, 8). This is God's exact promise to Abraham, and Abraham was careful to pass down the exact words of God's covenant to his inheritors.

This itself is a beautiful thing and we too can remind God of his promises towards us in our prayers. When you stand up and pray, remind God and tell him that He said: "Ask and you shall receive, seek and you shall find, knock and it shall be opened to you" (Mat 7:7) and "Whatever you ask in My name, that I will do, that the Father may be glorified in the Son" (John 14:13). Note that Jesus says, 'in My name', meaning that not every single earthly thing that we will ask for, we will receive. Instead, ask God for the comfort of the Holy Spirit, or the strength to overcome sin, and in His kindness and generosity, He will provide in abundance. Ultimately, what God desires and intends for us the most is our salvation, and thus whatever we ask God for with regards to our salvation, He will provide for us in abundance.

JOSEPH THE HUMBLE

Joseph brings his two children Ephraim and Manasseh, to receive blessing from Jacob. Notice the respect and reverence that Joseph treats his father with. In verse 12, Joseph "bows his face to the earth". Even though he lived as the second in charge of Egypt behind Pharaoh, he bowed towards his father in humility. He was of a much higher rank than his father, however, he bowed before his father because his nature was not proud. This teaches us an important lesson to "Honour your father and mother so that your days may be long on earth" (Ephesians 6: 2-3). Even if we believe our parents are wrong, restricting us, or treating us badly, there is a certain blessing that comes with offering them respect and obedience. And

What the Fathers Say

A wise son brings joy to his father, but a foolish son despises his mother

— Proverbs

Ephraim and Manasseh

In this chapter, Joseph presents his two children, Ephraim and Manasseh, to be blessed by Jacob. Jacob places his right hand upon Ephraim and his left hand upon Manasseh, indicating that Ephraim was to receive the greater blessing (even though he was younger). Why was this the case? Because Jacob knew and foretold that Ephraim would be greater than Manasseh. This was first realised in the census done in the time of Moses when 40, 500 men from the tribe of Ephraim would go to war, whilst only 22, 200 from the tribe of Manasseh were recruited (Numbers 1: 31, 33). Whilst the tribe of Manasseh was divided and mingled with pagan peoples and idol worshippers, the tribe of Ephraim produced great men and women like Joshua, Deborah, Gideon and Samuel. Preferring the younger than the older also refers to the coming of the second Adam (Christ), who occupied and reclaimed the birthright which the first Adam lost.

People, Places & Things

What the Fathers Say

There is no need at all to make long discourses; it is enough to stretch out one's hand and say: 'Lord as you will, and as you know, have mercy upon me'. And if the conflict grows fiercer, shout: 'Lord, help!'. God knows very much what we need and will show us His mercy

- Abba Macarius

even if we ever wrong them or argue, there is another blessing that comes with apologising and reconciling with them as well! Thus, we must strive to show honour and respect to our parents at all times. If even Jesus Himself obeyed His parents, and "was subject to them" (Luke 2:51), what is our excuse for our disobedience?

FAREWELL JACOB

Jacob is dying and then begins to say what could be termed as his "farewell speech". Jacob's final testimony is a testimony of grace, not personal merit. He does not mention that he was faithful to God, but rather that God has been faithful to Him. The phrase "God who fed me" (verse 15), literally means "God who shepherded me". Jacob does not make mention any of his achievements, but chooses to instead make mention of God's great mercy to him. We too, when we die, will not achieve anything if we have much success, a large family, lots of money or any other worldly thing- the grave is the same for the rich and the poor! The only thing that matters is our relationship with God.

This is the reason why monks and nuns decide to leave the world and pursue a relationship with God alone. They recognise the vanity of this world, and how futile everything is, and decide that a life with God is far better. St. Macarius even used to sleep with a skull next to him to remind him of his eventual death from the world! Now we are not all called to be monks and nuns, but we are called to make God the number one priority in our lives, to seek Him, and Him alone! Pope Shenouda even tells the story of a monk who was walking in the desert, busy in prayer. Suddenly, two angels appeared to him, one on his left, and the other on his right, but he did not even look at them. Why? Because he was so focused on the Lord, and refused to be distracted by anyone or anything else.

THE FINAL BLESSING

After this, Jacob blesses Ephraim and Manasseh, taking Ephraim with his right hand (the greater blessing), and Manasseh with his left (the lesser blessing). However, this displeases Joseph, who believes that Manasseh should receive more blessing because he is the eldest child. When Joseph attempts to rectify this, Jacob refuses because he knows exactly what he is doing and prophesies that even though he is younger, the nation of Ephraim will be a greater people than the people of Manasseh.

REFLECTION

Why do I disobey, argue and grumble against my parents? Let us learn from the example of Joseph, who honoured his father, even though he himself was of a much greater rank and status!

CHAPTER 49

JACOB BLESSES HIS SONS

In Jacob's final act as a patriarch and heir to Abraham and Isaac, he prophesies blessings upon each of his sons. However, some of these are not blessings, but rather prophesies about what will befall them in the future. This is the first conscious prophesy spoken by a man in the Bible. There were many prophesies announced by God before and many other veiled prophesies and interpretations of dreams, but this is the first one to be declared through the mouth of a man in the Bible. While we won't talk about every single prophesy directed to each son, we can learn a few important lessons from this chapter.

REUBEN: YOU SHALL NOT EXCEL

Jacob says to Reuben: "You shall not excel". Why? Because he went up to his father's bed, and defiled it. In other words, Reuben slept with his father's concubine (Gen 35:22). Notice that Reuben was the eldest, and that the eldest would usually receive blessing! But his impurity and inability to control his lustful passions, led him to be cursed. We know that not a single prophet, judge or king came from the line of Reuben, teaching us that the first can in fact become the last! This is a wakeup call for anyone struggling with sins of impurity including lustful glances, masturbation, unhealthy relationships, adultery, fornication or homosexuality. The sin of impurity is despised by God and has its

Events

CHAPTER 49

punishment on earth as well as in the second coming. God even destroyed the whole city of Sodom and Gomorrah because of its impurity!

SIMEON AND LEVI: I WILL SCATTER THEM IN ISRAEL

Another two sons and a different lesson to be learnt this time. Theses sons were also cursed, and received the same words for the same evil deeds. They were described as "instruments of cruelty", because they wiped out all the men of Shechem in retaliation for the rape of their sister Dinah (Gen 34: 25-29). At the time, Jacob did nothing to punish his children, other than registering a small and self-centred complaint (Gen 34:30). Yet God (and Jacob) did not forget this event. This teaches us that our past sins can come back to haunt us. Even if they are forgiven, they may bear consequences which last for a lifetime.

What the Fathers Say

If you are scorched by the fever of impurity, go to the banquet of the angels, and the spotless flesh of Christ will make you pure and chaste

– St. Cyril of Alexandria

Benjamin: a Ravenous Wolf?

Of Benjamin it was said: "Benjamin is a ravenous wolf. In the morning he shall devour the prey, and at night he shall divide the spoil: (Gen 49: 27). This prophesy refers to the courage of the tribe of Benjamin and its might in war. Of this tribe it was said: "Everyone of them could sling a stone at a hair's breadth and not miss" (Judges 20: 16). This prophesy is also believed to refer to King Saul, who was from the tribe of Benjamin, and threatened to devour King David like a wolf. It also refers to Saul of Tarsus (also from the tribe of Benjamin), who later became St. Paul. In the morning, Paul, the persecutor of the church, was like a wolf who devours. But in the evening, he became food to be offered, submitted to the Lamb.

People, Places &Things

JUDAH: WHOM HIS BROTHERS SHALL PRAISE

Jacob does not only offer negative prophesies, he also provides blessings upon those who have lived righteous lives as well! But Judah did not exactly live a righteous life. He suggested that Joseph his brother be sold for money (Gen 37:26), did not deal faithfully with Tamar (Gen 38:26) and even had sex with her when he looked at her as a prostitute (Gen 38: 18). But despite all this, he displayed good character when he interceded and offered himself as a substitute for Benjamin (Gen 44: 18-34). As such, God chose the tribe of Judah to bring forth the greatest sacrifice in the history of mankind, the Saviour Jesus Christ Himself. See how much God appreciates self-sacrifice! If God took the ultimate sacrifice for our sakes, it is only fitting that we sacrifice our time, pride, ego, money and absolutely everything for his sake as well.

GAD: HE SHALL TRIUMPH AT LAST

This is an interesting one. While God initially promises hardship to the tribe of Gad, he promises triumph at last. Initially, Jacob says "a troop shall trump upon him" and this came to pass when the foreign armies oppressed Gad (Jeremiah 49:1). However, victory would be his at the end and the tribe of Gad supplied many fine troops for David the king of Israel later on (1 Chron 12: 14). This is the promise that God gives many of his children, that darkness may come in the night, but light comes in the morning. Even if we face struggles with sins, trials or tribulations, we will win the battle if we are genuine in our prayer and repentance, and rise straight away every time we fall.

REFLECTION

Even if I am struggling with a particular sin which I just can't seem to get rid of, let us remember that weeping occurs in the night, but joy and victory will come in the morning!

Chapter 50

Events

CHAPTER 50

JACOB FINALLY DIES

In the final chapter of Genesis, two of the main characters of the book die. First Jacob, and later his son Joseph. In verse 1, Joseph falls on his father's face, weeps over him and kisses him. This is a very moving and dramatic scene, and since Jacob was a greatly honoured man, the whole nation of Egypt mourned 70 days over him. Not only this, but notice the detail with which the burial process is described in the book. The entire tribe gathered to pay tribute to the man who was the final link with the patriarchs. There is no burial recorded in the scriptures quite as honourable as this or with such wealth of detail.

Jacob's sons honour his death wish and bury him in the land of Canaan, exactly where he asked. Whilst they often opposed or disappointed him in life, they were extremely careful to honour him in his death. However, Joseph's brothers begin to fear that perhaps now that Jacob is dead, Joseph will begin to turn on them and repay them for all their evil deeds. Here they freely acknowledge all their wicked deeds, and are worried about justice. Joseph with his high status and prestige in Egypt, was certainly capable of executing any plan of revenge that he desired.

JOSEPH'S MERCY TO HIS BROTHERS

In verses 16-18, Joseph's brothers send messengers to Joseph, saying: "before your father died he commanded, please forgive the trespass of your brothers and their sin".

This story was probably made up, since there is no account in the Bible of this taking place. The brothers felt that they didn't have the right to ask Joseph for mercy, so they put the request for mercy in the mouth of their honourable and dead father. Now what was Joseph's response? Joseph wept (verse 17). Why would he weep? He probably wept because it seemed that his brothers thought so little of him and doubted his character so greatly. He wept because despite all that he had done for his brothers, they still thought he wanted to execute revenge upon him!

Joseph comforts his brothers and reassures them that he will not seek revenge or impose any punishment upon them? He questions his brothers; "Am I in the place of God" (verse 19), later telling them that "you meant evil against me, but God meant it for good" (verse 20). Every Christian should able to see the overarching and overruling hand of God in their life. No matter what evil

What the Fathers Say

Hope is a beacon of light to those who are living in darkness. It is a pillar of joy which comforts those who are saddened. It is the work of the Holy Spirit inside a person, the Spirit of Comfort which fills our hearts

– Pope Shenouda III

Joseph's Last Words

The book of Genesis begins with the creation of the world from nothing, and ends with Joseph's death and burial. This shows us the futility of life and that everything will eventually come to an end. Joseph, in his love for his brothers, comforted and reassured them saying: "Do not be afraid". He will not seek vengeance on them for their evil actions. He then informs them that God alone will be their provider, saying: "I am dying, but God will surely visit you and bring you out of this land, to the land which He swore to Abraham, Isaac and Jacob. This prophesy was realised at the hands of Moses and Joshua, who later lead the Israelites out of Egypt and into the Promised Land (read all about this in the book of Exodus!).

People, Places & Things

man may bring against us, God can use it for good. Joseph didn't have the text of Romans 8:28 "All things work together for good to those who love God" to comfort him in his hardships, but he had the truth of it. Sadly, many of us who have the text, do not have the truth.

A MESSAGE OF HOPE

There was an old priest who had the unique gift of ministering to the distressed and discouraged. In his Bible, he carried an old bookmark woven of silk threads into a motto. The back of it, where the threads were knotted and tied, was a hopeless tangle. He would take the bookmark out and show the troubled person the side of the bookmark and ask them to make sense of it. They never could. He would then turn it over, and on the front where white letters against a solid background, saying "God is love". When our life is tangled and meaningless, it is because we can see only one side of the tapestry.

To finish this book, it would be fitting to remember one last promise from the mouth of God: "Eye has not seen, nor ear heard. Nor have entered into the heart of man. The things which God has prepared for those who love Him" (1 Cor 2:9). No matter what happens in our life, we know that God is working. Even if we can't see it or understand it, we are His children and He only wants the best for us. We just have to believe, pray and follow the Sacraments! Many of the characters in the

Joseph grew greater, not by occupying the second place in Egypt after Pharaoh, but by the love that filled his heart; enjoying, not the righteousness of the law through keeping its commandments, but by following the evangelical law of love. He did not repay evil with evil, and did not even stop at forgiveness to those who wronged him. He could not bear to see their humiliation and wept bitterly. He did not even see their evil, but saw God's hand, which turned their evil into good

- Fr. Tadros Malaty

book of Genesis had weaknesses and faced various trials and tribulation. However, God, who is always faithful and never changes, is full of mercy, compassion and love and will never leave us.

REFLECTION

Am I close to giving up? Have I lost hope in myself for one reason or another? Let us remember that we have a merciful God, who is faithful and can fill even the most miserable soul with his divine hope!